For Those Being Crushed

Confronting our 'social justice' blind spot

Camilla Olim

**Kingdom
Publishers**

For Those Being Crushed
Copyright© Camilla Olim

All Scripture Quotations have been taken from the New International Version and the King James Version of the Bible.

ISBN: 978-1-913247-71-3

1st Edition by Kingdom Publishers
Kingdom Publishers
London, UK.

You can purchase copies of this book from any leading bookstore or email **contact@kingdompublishers.co.uk**

Dedication

In loving memory of Cindi Cooper.

Chapters

Acknowledgements

I want to say a brief thank you to those who have been part of making this project a reality.

Firstly, to my family – my wonderful parents, to Josh and Lindsey. You have been a source of constant support.

To Eleanor, my beautiful, vibrant best friend. This book was your idea. So much of the woman I am today is because of the way you've loved me like a sister over the years.

To the team at CBR UK, this book largely exists because of what I learnt from you. To Dave, a huge thank you for the generous amount of time and energy you have spent supporting me with this project.

To Regan and the trustees of Pregnancy Crisis Helpline, thank you for being such a joy to work with. You inspire me to no end.

To Andrea Williams, thank you for seeing something in 23-year-old me.

To the friends who supported me and cheered me on, even without being fully on board with this Jesus thing or this pro-life thing – a special thanks to you. Words don't cover how much that has meant to me.

To all who encouraged me and prayed for me over the years.

To the team at Kingdom Publishers, thank you for your service and for making this process so smooth.

And to the One who made me; the most faithful friend, loving Father and beautiful Saviour. To Him be all honour and glory and thanks.

Introduction

*"Speak up for those who cannot speak for themselves; ensure justice for those being crushed." – **Proverbs 31:8***

I started this book when I was a day shy of 26 years old; painfully aware that my life didn't look anything like how I imagined 26 to look. I haven't quite followed the tried-and-true. Or rather, more accurately, God would not let me follow the tried-and-true.

All things considered, despite the plot twists, the sacrifice and the hard slog, I truly believe it's better that way. I am becoming increasingly convinced that true freedom is only found in surrendering your life to the One who dreams over you – and who will call you higher, until your dreams echo His.

I've been writing since I was old enough to put pen to paper, and I hoped and dreamed that I would someday write a book. It never crossed my mind that I would write about abortion.

But in obedience, whether stumbling blind, being dragged kicking and screaming, or running full pelt, every step has somehow got me here; the inevitable meeting point of His heart and mine, of my dreams and His. Venturing out into the risky waters of pro-life activism means there's not much chance of a way back. Once you're out there dabbling in the shallows, there's only forward. What else can I do but continue to obey, with no certainty of the outcome? Can I stand before God one day and tell Him I tried to do a Jonah? I know that I can't tell Him I wasted the modicum of resource He gave me.

I'm not an expert in the medical field. I'm not a lawyer or a politician. I'm just a young woman whose heart has been burdened about a Goliath that must be taken down.

I first became truly aware of the abortion issue whilst working as a writer for campaign group Christian Concern. It was there that I attended the youth programme The Wilberforce Academy and was introduced to the work of the Centre for Bioethical Reform UK, for which I volunteer, particularly with its church-focused arm, Brephos. I am also a trustee for registered charity Pregnancy Crisis Helpline, and I have written several articles about the abortion issue on my personal blog, *The Accessible Christian*.

This book is an attempt to pen everything I have learned, observed and prayed about for the past few years.

1 John 4:19 states that, we love *"because He first loved us"*. I imagine the vast majority of those reading this will relate, to a greater or lesser extent, to struggling with low confidence, doubt and dependence on others' approval for validation. I'm certainly no exception. But a few years ago I experienced a tough season that I believe shaped me for the rest of my life. We all suffer by degrees and at some point, if we're

serious enough about following Christ, we will go through what some refer to as the 'dark night of the soul'. I suppose this period in my life was mine. I remember during this time I felt like I was being kicked repeatedly. Each time I tried to get back on my feet, I'd get kicked again harder, until, after two years of this, I felt completely and utterly broken; Rock bottom; A few steps short of a complete nervous breakdown.

There were so many lessons I learned during that time but there was no harder or more important lesson than to learn to worship God solely for whom He is instead of as a response to my circumstances. I learnt how to lean into God's heart and know friendship with Him, especially during times when all human comfort fell short and I had no-one but God to turn to. In the testing fire of my own disappointments and trials, and in the exposing of my own weaknesses, I finally began to see God as a warrior who was totally committed to my holiness, to my freedom, and to my thriving. When I began to comprehend just how fiercely the Lord would fight for me, my own insecurities began to fade. My need to please and to have everyone like and approve of me lessened a little (which is just as well, because involvement with the pro-life movement will not make you popular – not even amongst fellow Christians).

I am not completely cured of people-pleasing and I am not fully secure in myself – who could honestly say they were? Sometimes the fear of man rears its ugly head again, and like most people, I like to be liked. To be completely honest and human with you, there are still times when I would rather I were called to anything else but to speak about abortion. I've been tempted more than once to just abandon the whole thing and live a 'normal' life. I'd be more comfortable, I'd have more friends, and I wouldn't cause offence. I won't say I sailed through this without an ounce of bitterness; that the rejection of man was water off a duck's back. Instead, it's been a process of forgiving and re-forgiving, of constantly having to take these things to Jesus.

But on the whole, I am still freer today than I have ever been. I am more content and at peace with myself than I have ever been and it is only down to the unrelenting love of God, who shows Himself strong in my human weakness. It is from this place of growing freedom that I was able to write this book.

As obvious as writing this may seem to me now, it wasn't actually my idea, but rather the suggestion of my best friend. I am forever grateful to her for pointing out what to her was most obvious – but what I was blind to. We all have blind spots, after all.

The global Holocaust

"Action is the only remedy to indifference: the most insidious danger of all."[1] So said Elie Wiesel, human rights activist and Nobel Peace Prize winner. Wiesel, who had survived the horrors of the Jewish Holocaust, knew first-hand the terrible cost of apathy; so much so that he devoted the rest of his life

---

[1] *Time* [online] Available at: https://time.com/4392267/elie-wiesel-dead-nobel-peace-prize-speech/ [Accessed 12 Oct. 2019].

to humanitarian causes. Wiesel believed it is the duty of mankind to interfere when evil is at hand.

Do we?

Though it is uncomfortable to accept, we are living in the era of the global Holocaust.

Behind closed doors, silenced and sterilised, the greatest mass-killing (dare I even say genocide) in human history is taking place. Like the Africans brutally shipped across the ocean and sold during the Transatlantic slave trade; like the Jewish people carted into concentration camps and disposed of in gas chambers, the victims of this atrocity are kept out of sight, dehumanised and euphemised. Such ugliness is not fit for the eyes of ordinary citizens.

It is a unique kind of genocide, if it can so be called, because it is not restricted to a single geographical location, race, gender or class. While some victims are at greater risk than others, no single sub-sector of this group is totally exempt.

The primary victims (for there are secondary and tertiary and a whole chain of further victims), are the unborn. Not 'pregnancies'; not 'tissue' or 'clumps of cells'. Living human beings, separate, whole and distinct from their mothers from the moment of fertilisation.

In the UK alone, 1 in 5 lives in the womb are ended; around 800 every working day. That's akin to the same number of daily deaths in the UK at the height of the COVID-19 pandemic.

In 2019, the highest ever number of abortions in England and Wales was recorded, at 207,384.[2] And 98% of these deaths are funded by you, the taxpayer, via the NHS.

Since the 1967 Abortion Act, over 9 million lives are missing from the UK, as a result of abortion. If you can imagine the entire population of London wiped from existence, you have a rough idea of just how high that number is. Or to contextualise that number another way, just fewer than 1 million lives were lost in the UK as a result of the First World War. Abortion has claimed 9 times that many lives.

At the time of writing this, the British Pregnancy Advisory Service, Britain's leading abortion provider, continues with the backing of certain MPs to push its campaign to decriminalise abortion, effectively removing current protections that safeguard against abortion on demand. In July 2019 the abortion lobby succeeded in a cunning and completely undemocratic ploy to sneak abortion into Northern Ireland by the back door. 'The most pro-life country in the UK has now become the most destructive as abortion was legalised, for any reason, for up to 28 weeks' gestation.[3].

Meanwhile Labour MP Stella Creasy has spearheaded a push to see this echoed in the rest of the UK- and has denounced

---

[2] Department of Health and Social Care. *Abortion Statistics for England and Wales: 2019. GOV.UK*, GOV.UK, 11 June 2020. Available at: https://www.gov.uk/government/statistics/abortion-statistics-for-england-and-wales-2019

[3] Amnesty.org.uk. (2019). *Northern Ireland: 'historic day' as abortion ban lifted and equal marriage made law*. [online] Available at: https://www.amnesty.org.uk/press-releases/northern-ireland-historic-day-abortion-ban-lifted-and-equal-marriage-made-law [Accessed 6 Oct. 2019].

attempts[4] to show the public what exactly this would look like for the unborn as 'intimidation and harassment'.

In the midst of the 2020 Coronavirus pandemic, the long-discussed 'DIY abortions' have finally become a reality, after the UK government did a double U-turn to allow women to take the abortion pill at home, without medical supervision. Concerns have been raised by the government about the practice of sex-selective abortions[5], yet around 9 in 10 unborn babies diagnosed prenatally with Down's syndrome are aborted[6] without similar outcry. Moral relativism is running riot and our country's position is becoming ever more extreme. Dressed in choice-focused, woman-focused rhetoric, abortion slowly ingrains itself further into society's very fabric, to the point where it is difficult to imagine life without it. In the eyes of pro-abortion campaigners, abortion is a woman's 'right'. In the eyes of the NHS, abortion is 'healthcare'. And so we are stumbling half-blind towards an almost complete acceptance of this practice.

As a nation, in the name of 'choice', we are condoning the mass destruction of the most vulnerable members of our

---

[4] Centre for Bio-Ethical Reform UK. (2019). *#StopStella Campaign*. [online] Available at: https://www.cbruk.org/stopstella [Accessed 9 Oct. 2019].
[5] BBC News. (2019). *Labour: Ban early baby sex tests*. [online] Available at: https://www.bbc.co.uk/news/health-45497454 [Accessed 6 Oct. 2019].
[6] The National Down Syndrome Cytogenetic Register for England and Wales:
2009 Annual Report: (2019). [online] Available at:
http://archive.wolfson.qmul.ac.uk/ndscr/reports/NDSCRreport09. pdf

society. We are condoning the sacrifice of the weakest for the sake of the strong.

Pause for a moment and let that sink in.

Now, stay with me – don't throw the book across the room just yet.

I fully understand that abortion is an ugly word carrying a lot of emotional and uncomfortable connotations. We probably all have at least one story of being directly or indirectly affected by abortion, and so it is nearly impossible to approach this topic without some degree of mess. So in picking up this book, you've committed an act of courage already.

It may be that the very word makes you inwardly recoil. Perhaps it is associated with difficult decisions made by you or somebody close to you. Perhaps the word fills you with frustration and anger because you've witnessed the issue being handled poorly.

Maybe the word 'abortion' brings up images of America – a country where this issue is much more openly discussed – and therefore, more obviously divisive and more overtly politicised. You envision protests and counter-protests; Picketing, slogans, lots of anger, lots of conflict.

Maybe you read the title of this book and sighed at the thought of yet another ethical handbook, or another treatise on lobbying the government. Those things are necessary but there are probably enough of those already in existence.

So it may be best to begin by highlighting what this book is not.

This book is not primarily a resource on pro-life apologetics. If that's what you're after, there are much better resources out there – I'd recommend *'Why Pro-Life?'* by Randy Alcorn, *'The Case for Life'* by Scott Klusendorf and *'Matters of Life and Death'* by John Wyatt to really cement a proper understanding of the pro-life position. These people are far more qualified to discuss this at length than I am.

And although I will touch on public policy because it is necessary to this discussion, I am not a lawyer or a lobbyist, and this book is not primarily designed to persuade you to campaign to make abortion illegal. (Yes, you read that correctly).

This book, it must also be made explicitly clear from the outset, is not intended to shame or condemn any woman who has had an abortion, or any man who has been complicit in an abortion decision. Please hear my heart right from the beginning: no matter who you are and what you have done, I write this book in love. I hope you will read through this book in the knowledge that when Jesus died on that cross, He paid for ALL sin. He died and rose again to forgive all who repent and to restore all that is broken.

You may be wondering, what is there left to say?

This book is about the heart of God.

This book is for the Church.

Perhaps you consider this to be redundant – the Church's position on abortion is crystal clear, isn't it? Surely a whole book dedicated to this gritty subject is just preaching to the choir; one more tired voice bouncing around an echo-chamber.

Well, judging by my own experience, the anecdotes of others, and most importantly actual data, this simply isn't the case. And our lack of unity and conviction - our very blindness, in fact - is costing lives.

This book, then, is a passionate plea for the Bride of Christ to confront, in all sobrieties, the effects of our complicity. It is a plea for the Church to faithfully, compassionately and courageously engage in this most fierce and pressing of spiritual battles, and hopefully, to go some way towards helping you understand how. I hope that regardless of your current beliefs, background or experience, you will find something valuable in this book. My prayer is that God may use even a fraction of my imperfect words to stir us up as a united voice; so that we would not only engage in the fight, but in Christ's victory, win.

What do I mean by win? I mean that abortion would become unthinkable; an outcome I truly believe is possible. What would it take to get us there? In the following chapters, I aim to take you on a figurative journey towards making this happen. I aim to show you that you can become an effective agent of change, starting with the first courageous steps of individual transformation through alignment with the Word of God and understanding God's heart on this issue. I want to show you how corporately, we can learn from our past silence in the face of other injustices we now roundly condemn, and how a united and convicted Church body can have extraordinary impact on society. I want to consider the ongoing cost of our silence in light of the current trajectory our nation is travelling in. Finally, I aim to show you that if we employ Heaven's strategies and take seriously God's commands, we can reasonably hope to see the tide turn.

Finally, a brief note: I'm using this preamble to offer a short disclaimer (which I wish wasn't necessary but I fear in today's outrage-based climate, is). I will reference a number of writers and personalities in this book. My quoting or citing these individuals does not necessarily equate to my endorsing all of their views. I hope that regardless of your theological or political persuasions, you will be able to read these quotes and judge them on their own merit.

Chapter 1: The Heart of God

*"So God created mankind in his own image,
in the image of God he created them;
male and female he created them."* Genesis 1:27

There is no-where to begin but at the beginning. There are plenty of good scientific and philosophical arguments against abortion, and I strongly believe that having a basic grasp of these is important when it comes to discussing abortion with others. But all of science comes from God. And of course, morality comes from God – as His image-bearers, His law is written on our hearts (Romans 2:15). Regardless of where we are on the timeline of history; regardless of where the moral goalposts shift, God's eternal standard is stamped onto our very being. So we must first be convinced that this matters to God, before it can really matter to us at all.

The fact that God created us in His own image is a source of never-ending wonder to me. There are over 7 billion of us, all walking around bearing the essence of the Creator of the Universe – some, deeply acquainted with this Creator – others, totally estranged from Him. But all of us loved infinitely in spite of our sinful state, by One who knew no fault.

The value placed on us by the One who breathed galaxies into existence is too great for the human mind to comprehend, but Scripture certainly gives us some inkling of just how significant we are.

Life begins at the moment of fertilisation – this is scientifically correct, and the Bible confirms it. In Psalm 51:5, when repenting of adultery and murder, King David reflects, *"Surely I was sinful at birth, sinful from the time my mother conceived me"*; he recognised that personhood begins at the moment of conception.

But God dreamed you up before that. Before you *were*, the God who exists outside of space and time knew you and wanted you. The familiar Psalm 139 is a beautiful picture of David's recognition of this: *"Your eyes saw my unformed body; all the days ordained for me were written in your book before one of them came to be."*

And the Lord tells the young prophet Jeremiah: *"Before I formed you in the womb I knew you"*. (Jeremiah 1:5). In Galatians 1:15 Paul speaks of being *"set apart from [his] mother's womb"*.

Long before science confirmed it, these men of millennia past understood that life's value is not determined by size, environment, and level of development or degree of dependency. They understood in fact that God values life before its very conception. Indeed, the same Greek word is used in the Bible to describe a born child and an unborn child

– *'brephos'*. If the unborn child is human, as science and the Bible unequivocally demonstrate, then the unborn is our neighbour.

These men understood something of God's heart that is fundamental in our grasp of the significance of abortion: That our God is a Father who knows His children intimately before they have taken their first breath. There is not one life that our Father does not dream over. It is not the intention of this book to engage in a theological debate over sovereignty or predestination, but I believe the heart of God desires every life to be lived – and in turn, to glorify its Maker (Ephesians 2:10).

This means no life, 'planned' or 'unplanned', wanted or unwanted, healthy or sick, is a mistake to God.

Think of the popular worship song *'No Longer Slaves'*. There's a reason this song is so popular – it's packed with profound biblical truth; truth worth rejoicing in. The lines we tend to focus on, of course, are the chorus lines – *"I'm no longer a slave to fear; I am a child of God."*[7] Yet how often do we stop to meditate on this line – *"From my mother's womb you have chosen me; love has called my name"*? This is almost a direct quote from the apostle Paul himself. How many times have we sung this without stopping to wonder at its significance?

---

[7] Helser, J., Johnson, B. and Case, J. (2015). *No Longer Slaves*. [CD] Bethel Music.

No matter how a child is conceived, to be chosen and called from the very womb means that to God, no life is unwanted, unloved or unworthy.

It's not so difficult, then, to imagine the pain it causes our Father to see lives ripped from the womb before they experience a single day in the outside world. His grief and heartbreak over the wilful destruction of human beings bearing His image cannot be overemphasised – certainly, our own outrage could never match it.

Modern-day child sacrifice

If you remain unconvinced that a loving Father could be wrathful about abortion, consider the penalty for harming a pregnant woman's unborn child in Old Testament law: *"If people are fighting and **hit a pregnant woman and she gives birth prematurely** but there is no serious injury, the offender must be fined whatever the woman's husband demands and the court allows. **But if there is serious injury,** you are to take life for life, eye for eye, tooth for tooth, hand for hand, foot for foot, burn for burn, wound for wound, bruise for bruise."* (Exodus 21:22-25, emphasis mine).

And consider His response to the horrendous practice of child sacrifice to the Ammonite god Molech. Statues of Molech were often built out of bronze, and the arms, outstretched, were made red-hot by a fire pit below. The Ammonites placed babies into the arms of Molech as living sacrifices.

In Leviticus, God's warning to the Israelites to abstain from this evil practice could hardly be clearer:

> "Say to the Israelites: **'Any Israelite or any foreigner residing in Israel who sacrifices any of his children to Molek is to be put to death.** The members of the community are to stone him. I myself will set my face against him and will cut him off from his people; for by sacrificing his children to Molek, he has defiled my sanctuary and profaned my holy name. If the **members of the community close their eyes** when that man sacrifices one of his children to Molek and if they fail to put him to death, **I myself will set my face against him and his family** and will cut them off from their people together with all who follow him in prostituting themselves to Molek.'" (Leviticus 20:2-5, emphasis mine).

God is shown here to be both heartbroken Father and Righteous Judge, demanding action, not passivity, in the face of evil. This passage demonstrates not only the seriousness of child sacrifice to the Lord – few sins in the Bible provoke such a drastic response from Him - but the seriousness of turning a blind eye to it. Consider the outrage caused by the uncovering of child sex abuse scandals – added to the horror of the abuse itself, we feel disgust and anger at those in power who chose to look the other way instead of intervene.

In Jeremiah, the Lord speaks of the people of Judah who committed child sacrifice: *"They built the high places of Baal in the Valley of the Son of Hinnom, to offer up their sons and daughters to Molech, though I did not command them, **nor*** *did it enter into my mind, that they should do this abomination, to cause Judah to sin."* (Jeremiah 32:25)

The magnitude of this barbarism was such that it hadn't even crossed God's mind.

Though uncomfortable to entertain, there is certainly a case for abortion being a modern-day version of child sacrifice. It is, at its heart, the sacrificing of human life on the altar of convenience and comfort; or even as a means to attempt to escape deep personal suffering, such as in the rare cases of abortion on the grounds of rape. By saying this, I do not intend to dismiss this suffering, gloss over it or trivialise it, and I hope to discuss it at greater length in later chapters. But it is still a kind of sacrifice - not as openly barbaric or as clearly defined as what the Ammonites did to their children, but nonetheless, in both cases an exchange is intended.

Consider this in contrast with the life of Jesus. If there can be any remaining doubt as to the worth of the unborn child, remember first that Jesus affirmed the humanity of the unborn child by becoming one. And the first person to recognise Jesus, himself yet a growing foetus, was another unborn child: his cousin, John the Baptist: *"At that time Mary got ready and hurried to a town in the hill country of Judea, where she entered Zechariah's home and greeted Elizabeth. When Elizabeth heard Mary's greeting, **the baby leaped in her womb**, and Elizabeth was filled with the Holy Spirit."* (Luke 1:39-41).

In her commentary of Mary's call to carry the Christ, *Mary's Story, Mary's Song,* Elaine Storkey writes: *"[Elizabeth's] baby relates to the sound of Mary's greeting, and to the presence of Mary's own infant. The movement of this baby is a leap of joy. It is the recognition that although his eyes cannot see not his lungs yet breathe this baby knows he is in the very presence of God. The Holy Spirit discloses to this unborn child that what is developing in the womb of Mary is none other than the coming Messiah."*[8] It is extraordinary to consider that today we grant the foetus so little worth and so few rights, yet John the Baptist as a developing foetus was able both to recognise and extol the Living God.

The value that Jesus placed on children also cannot be overstated, rebuking his disciples for trying to stop parents bringing their children to Him: *"When Jesus saw this, he was indignant. He said to them, "Let the little children come to me, and do not hinder them, for the kingdom of God belongs to such as these."* (Mark 10:14). And His warning about those who would corrupt the youngest is stark: *"But if anyone causes one of these little ones who believe in Me to stumble, it would be better for him to have a large millstone hung around his neck and to be thrown into the sea."* (Mark 9:42)

Finally, Jesus Himself modelled the antithesis of abortion. Whilst men and women sacrifice unborn lives for their own gain, Jesus sacrificed His own life in exchange for ours. We inflict violent, bloody death on innocent human beings; Jesus allowed violent, bloody death to be inflicted upon Him for sinful humanity. Nothing exposes the evil of abortion more completely than the very image of Christ on that gnarled wooden cross.

---

[8] Storkey, E., 1993. *Mary's Story, Mary's Song*. London: Fount, pp.39-40.

Although the Bible may not say much about abortion, there is certainly enough material to make God's position on it totally unambiguous. If it moves the heart of God, it should move us accordingly. Dr Calum Miller, who teaches Bioethics at the Oxford Centre for Christian Apologetics, writes on his blog: *"Some things aren't mentioned explicitly in the Bible because they weren't common cultural problems or because they are covered by other commands. The Bible doesn't mention female genital mutilation (FGM) because it wasn't common in Hebrew culture. Likewise, because the culture was very pro-life and in particular valued having children, abortion was not a common problem (bear in mind how much pride people in the [Old Testament] took in having many children, and how much of a curse lacking children was seen as)."*[9]

FGM isn't mentioned in the Bible, but if asked, I imagine most of us could quite easily explain why it's wrong, based on our understanding of the Bible's foundational moral principles. We can piece together a picture of God's heart towards abortion in the same way.

Knowing love so we can love

The very fact that the lives of the unborn are so precious and valuable to God is key in understanding why abortion is so widespread. As image-bearers of God, Satan hates humanity.

---

[9] Miller, C. (2018). *Jesus and the early church on abortion*. [online] Available at: https://calumsblog.com/2018/12/07/jesus-church-abortion/ [Accessed 9 Oct. 2019].

As I heard Professor John Wyatt put it once, he hates every human being because they remind him of the King. So naturally, he loves abortion. He comes to steal, to kill and destroy, and he loves to watch us willingly destroy one another and debase what God has lovingly created. He loves to see families torn apart; men and women scarred.

This is a raging spiritual war and we are required to act.

A seemingly overwhelming task, you might think. Where to even begin?

May I humbly suggest that you begin by allowing yourself to be moved? Not, in the first instance, by abortion – we'll get to that – but firstly by the love of God, for *"We love because He first loved us"* (1 John 4:19). This has certainly been true for me. Before I could be fully gripped by the necessity to speak of the value of others, I needed to first have some inkling of my own. Of course, it starts with the cross – the simple knowledge of the gospel. And through the cross we can know relationship with the One who designed us for intimacy.

If you do not understand your own value, you will never be mobilised to go to any great lengths to defend the value of another – especially an invisible, totally defenceless other. God will use whatever you offer Him, it's true. But a life unfettered is doubtless more effective than one hampered by struggles Jesus died to set you free from.

Some are familiar with Maslow's hierarchy of needs – the idea that only when man reaches 'self-actualization'; that is, only when he has all his basic needs met and desires fulfilled, can he turn outwards and engage with morality and problem-solving. Perhaps there is some practical truth in that. But in the Kingdom of God, things don't always seem to work this way. For it was out of my lack that I submitted to God. In the midst of my darkest season that, on my knees, I promised the Lord I would, in some capacity, fight for the unborn child for the rest of my life. I understood in that darkness that I mattered, and if I mattered, so did they. I wake up grateful now for the honour of getting to share his heart for the unborn.

Not everyone is called to become a full-time pro-life activist. But the principle remains the same. If you struggle with your own self-worth, run to Jesus. Run to the foot of the cross. You must understand that you are loved in order to truly love.

Chapter 2: Confronting discomfort

"You may choose to look the other way but you can never say again that you did not know." – **William Wilberforce**

Tragedy is inescapable, and in today's climate of constant connection, it is overwhelming. How many times have you switched channels, turned the page or closed the app, swamped by sadness and powerlessness over some event that's just too big for you? I have many times, especially during periods when I was struggling to cope with events in my own life.

It's no wonder, really. Life may not be as precarious (at least in the West) as it was even a century ago – but it's still hard. Suffering is inevitable and there is only so much the human heart can take. In his bestselling book *12 Rules for Life: An Antidote to Chaos,* clinical psychologist and Professor of Psychology Jordan Peterson writes: *"Humanity, in toto, and those who compose it as identifiable people deserve some sympathy for the appalling burden under which the human individual genuinely staggers; some sympathy for subjugation to mortal vulnerability, tyranny of the state, and the depredations of nature."*[10]

There is only One who has the capacity for such a daunting task as to shoulder the burden of the entire world, and He has already done it. Take heart, He says – *"I have overcome the world"*. (John 16:33). This reminder certainly brings me comfort in the face of observing the depth of corruption and suffering across the globe.

But there is another side to the coin. For just as we were not designed to bear the world's burdens, neither were we destined to escape all suffering and live a life of ease and self-gratification.

While suffering is inescapable for everyone, for followers of Christ it's part of what we sign up for. There is no way a true disciple of Jesus can live in total comfort and ease. That was not promised us. Instead, we've been promised suffering, persecution and hardship for our obedience to Him, and the early followers of Jesus knew this all too well. Paul writes in 2 Timothy 3:12, *"Indeed, all who desire to live a godly life in Christ Jesus will be persecuted"*. In 2 Corinthians 12:10, he says: *"For the sake of Christ, then, I am content with weaknesses, insults, hardships, persecutions, and calamities."*

I recognise that in the West, we are not experiencing the persecution faced by our brothers and sisters in other parts of the world, nor the kind the apostles endured. We are not

---

[10] Peterson, Jordan B, *12 Rules for Life, An Antidote to Chaos,* Random House Canada, 2019. p.61

living in fear of our very lives. Thankfully, we are not imprisoned or barred from gathering to worship.

Yet if we face any kind of opposition for obedience to Christ it should not come as a shock. Some believers are experiencing reprimands, fines and even bars to office for the outworking of their faith in a public space – *The Christian Legal Centre* has dozens of examples of cases like this.

But even in a relatively persecution-free West, to be promised suffering itself is hardly attractive. In our society stuffed to the brim with self-medication, it sounds downright appalling.

You're probably self-medicating without even realising it. I'm not just talking about booze or porn. Even if you find your comfort in Netflix or chocolate or music or the gym, you self-medicate.

I'm no exception to this and I am not suggesting that all of these are bad things in themselves. But we have become used to reaching for comfort, to softening the harshness of life and escaping things we do not like.

Jesus promised to send us the Holy Spirit – the Comforter – because we were not designed to live wholly comfortable. Truly obeying Jesus' commands will mean venturing out into the realm of the risky, the painful and the disturbing.

I am encouraged to see that in many ways, the Church is doing this so well. The Church's involvement with projects tackling various social issues is to be applauded. I thank God for the ways His people stand in the gap every single day for vulnerable people from all walks of life.

Are we willing to wade into uncomfortable waters when it comes to abortion too?

Rude awakening

In Chapter 1 I scratched the surface of God's heart for the unborn child. When we come to grips with the gravity of this issue – when we can no longer pretend this is not of utmost priority to the One we worship – then it follows that we allow our own hearts to be changed.

My own concept of abortion was vague growing up. I have blurred memories of reading a big pink hardback book at my parents' house that included illustrations of babies developing in the womb. I have some recollection of it mentioning abortion but in my young mind, I couldn't comprehend it. As I grew older, the subject was left on the sidelines of my consciousness. I knew abortion meant a child in the womb died, but I couldn't tell you how. In my ignorance, I imagined it was some sort of gentle vanishing – a wand waved and poof, baby disappears.

Despite reading that pink book as a child, I didn't remember much about foetal development – that a foetus has a heartbeat at 21 days; that at eight weeks a foetus's facial features are beginning to develop. That at 12 weeks a foetus can close his or her fist.

In the UK, it is legal to have abortions up to 24 weeks, with some in the abortion lobby campaigning for no upper limit at all.

When I turned 23, fresh out of university waving around my Humanities degree and as clueless as they come, I started working at Christian Concern, an organisation that engaged, amongst other tough issues, with bioethics. It was a rude awakening. Not only did I realise that I didn't really know anything, despite the volume of books I'd consumed during my four-year degree; I also realised that I could no longer continue being a Christian and remain on the fence about what I truly believed. For the first time, I was forced to confront what before was shrouded in mystery. It wasn't just the basic biology of foetal development that I had to contend with. During my first couple of weeks in that job I attended a talk which included the showing of a video depicting a real surgical abortion. That was the turning point. From then on, I could not go back to my comfortable ignorance. I could not erase the horror of what I had seen.

Before then, like some of you, I did not know that during second-trimester D&E abortions, foetuses are ripped limb from limb from the womb. I didn't know that their skulls are crushed. I didn't know that third trimester abortions involve injecting the child with a drug that stops their heart and then having the mother deliver the baby dead. Now I know these statements are not scare-mongering tools from the pro-life lobby, but facts. Now I know, and I cannot pretend I do not know.

It was education that changed my outlook from one of mild concern to a conviction that I must act. It was the visual evidence of these acts of violence that shook me out of passivity; that impressed upon me the humanity of the unborn at any stage of development and the sheer barbarism of wilfully destroying them.

Learning to see

There's something to be said for the use of images – in fact, they've been at the heart of social reform for a long time. Wilberforce could not have achieved the abolition of slavery in the UK without the illustrations and props used by Thomas Clarkson and his associates. The Civil Rights Movement was largely sparked by the image of Emmett Till, a teenage African-American murdered simply because he was black. After the ending of the Second World War, German citizens were taken to the Holocaust death camps to see with their own eyes the utter horror of what had taken place under their noses. Regardless of whether you think abortion is a comparable injustice to these other shocking events in history, the primary lesson is this: Visuals help to provoke the emotional response in us necessary to shift our perspective and drive home truth.

Martin Luther King Jr. put it so eloquently in his renowned *Letter from Birmingham Jail: "Like a boil that can never be cured so long as it is covered up but must be opened with all its ugliness to the natural medicines of air and light, injustice must be exposed, with all the tension its exposure creates, to the light of human conscience and the air of national opinion before it can be cured."[11]*

The use of abortion imagery has provoked plenty of outrage in the public space, and I would argue that this has less to do with our aversion to violence (we happily expose ourselves to all kinds of violent material) than it has to do with the pinprick of our national conscience.

You may not believe that abortion imagery belongs in the public domain, and it is not the purpose of this book to convince you that it does. But if you have never, privately or otherwise, viewed one of these images, I would recommend – urge, even – that you bring yourself to do so. In the same way that the Holocaust likely seemed incomprehensible to you until you saw the photographs in your history textbook, so will abortion become very real to you upon seeing it.

Dare to look at what society has hidden for 50 years. Let the image speak for itself. I know very well that words alone are inadequate.

That isn't to say that words hold no power. In fact, in order to comprehend how as a society we have allowed this, language provides much of the answer. As an English Literature graduate, I take a natural interest in the power of language – but it was during my time working at Christian Concern that my eye was trained to spot intentional use of language to redefine, influence and even manipulate.

---

[11] Luther King Jr, M. (n.d.). *Letter from a Birmingham Jail [King, Jr.]* [online] Africa.upenn.edu. Available at:
https://www.africa.upenn.edu/Articles_Gen/Letter_Birmingham.html
[Accessed 9 Oct. 2019].

In fact, even my Holy Grail first-year student textbook, *'An Introduction to Literature, Criticism and Theory'*, asserts: *"Ideology, the way that people think about their world, is produced and altered in and through language. Language changes, and even creates the social and political world in which we live".*[12]

Narratives are crafted, not merely relayed. Even the media outlets, that you grew up believing were impartial, carefully mould and shape the story they want to tell according to the cultural zeitgeist. And when it comes to abortion, the fiercest and most contentious of debates, words hold enormous sway. Think about the times you've heard abortion being discussed in the media, amongst your colleagues or classmates. How were these discussions framed? Perhaps slogans like 'My body, my choice' come to mind. Perhaps you think of phrases like 'reproductive rights' or 'women's healthcare'; words like 'foetus' (which by the way is just Latin for offspring); 'clump of cells', 'termination', 'tissue'.

Have you noticed that UK news providers always refer to pro-life endeavours as 'anti-abortion' or even 'anti-choice'? Some go further – it's common to see (usually old, white, religious) men being blamed for 'trying to control women's bodies'. I once even saw an article on the Guardian website about how pro-life supporters were actually 'pro-death'!

Or have you noticed how the language surrounding the unborn is completely altered depending on whether the child is wanted or not? 'Smoking harms your unborn baby', warn

---

[12] Bennett, A. and Royle, N. (2014). An Introduction to Literature, Criticism and Theory. Hoboken: Taylor and Francis, p.199.

cigarette packets. Headlines were made in 2018 when doctors performed surgery on unborn *babies* with spina bifida – not on 'products of conception'! And would you congratulate a happy expectant mother on her growing foetus? Would you ask her if she'd felt the foetus kick yet?

How many times have you heard this disparate terminology and not stopped to question it? It's a distinct possibility that you have been conditioned to accept abortion as. At worst, it's an inevitable part of some people's lives, and at best, a positive, empowering option for women. You may even sympathise with the view that any attempt to restrict legal access to abortion is an attack on women; a show of misogyny and control.

Put simply, the abortion lobby has dehumanised the unborn child. That is how society has become comfortable with their mass destruction.

This isn't new. Systemic injustice has always succeeded through the dehumanisation of its victims. Western civilisation justified the slave trade on the basis that black people were sub-human. Hitler slaughtered six million Jews by convincing an entire nation that Jews were no better than rats or pigs. Elie Wiesel said at the opening of the Holocaust History Museum in 2005: *"Jews were not killed because they were human beings. In the eyes of the killers they were not human beings! They were Jews!"*[13]

---

[13] Yadvashem.org. *Echoes & Reflections: Speech by Elie Wiesel - Education & E-Learning - Yad Vashem.* [online] Available at:

It is frightening how easy it is for image-bearers of God to dehumanise fellow image-bearers of God.

The mass killing of the unborn is also systemic and as a moral act it is no better than any of the horrors I just mentioned.

Interestingly, even controversial political commentator Milo Yiannopoulos stated in a 2019 interview with Christian radio host, author and Professor Dr. Michael Brown: *"It all boils down to abortion… that's why abortion is the central and most important issue, politically, in the U.S – because it's the most important issue for humanity; it's the most important issue **there is**. Do human beings have intrinsic moral worth or not?"*[14]

Yet we as a society, and more pointedly the Church, are largely unconcerned, and this is demonstrated in our lack of response.

God's heart for the unborn and His anger at their destruction is absolutely incompatible with our apathy. If we call ourselves his disciples, then it is imperative that we identify where we've accepted and adopted lies about abortion, and instead confront some painful truths.

What truths? Well, firstly, the ugly truth about what abortion is? How it works and what it looks like? And then observe the

---

https://www.yadvashem.org/yv/en/education/educational_materials/adl/lesson5_speech.asp [Accessed 12 Oct. 2019]

[14] YouTube. (2019). *MILO: The Demonic Roots of Abortion*. [online] Available at: https://www.youtube.com/watch?v=XSnsJKD9W3k [Accessed 16 Oct. 2019].

mind-bendingly stark contrast between this reality and the sterile and benign way we, as a society, frame this evil.

This may be difficult at first. It's much easier to believe in society's inherent goodness and believe that everything I've told you about abortion is nothing more than sensationalising to try and 'get you on my side'. It's easier to dismiss me as a fundamentalist or an extremist; a woman utterly lacking in compassion for her fellow females. Because it's easier to believe that than to acknowledge that there might be something rotten at the heart of our society.

I won't sugar-coat this: If you come to God with a soft, open and tender heart, and for the first time brace yourself for the truth about abortion, you will be haunted by what you see. You won't be able to forget it, and it will weigh upon your conscience. If you decide to act on what you have seen – even by the smallest act of vocal dissent – you will probably be criticised, laughed at and scorned.

The easier thing is usually not the right thing. But who would you rather displease? Man or your Maker? Choose this day whom will you serve.

For you may find that if you climb this hurdle of discomfort and allow God to break your heart over abortion, the suffering isn't so bad. Jesus says we should be called blessed when we are *"persecuted because of righteousness"*; when others *"insult you and persecute you and falsely say all kind of evil against you because of me. Rejoice,"* he says, *"and be glad, for your reward is great in heaven, for so they persecuted the prophets who were before you."* (Matthew 5:10-12).

In *Seeing Jesus from the East* by Ravi Zacharias and Abdu Murray, Murray encourages us with the promise that alongside suffering for the sake of Christ, we can experience great joy. *"So many around the world have demonstrated their willingness to live like [Paul]. Why? Not because any one of us is braver than the next person, but because each of us has discovered that suffering for Christ isn't the only thing that is inevitable; so are His blessings. When we see that, we won't just be willing to experience pain; we may be eager to."*[15]

There's a joy in tasting the suffering of Jesus that surpasses any earthly comfort. Hebrews 12:2 says Jesus Himself endured the cross *"for the joy set before Him."* Will we take up our cross? Will we endure it for the joy of knowing Him?

Please, if you haven't already, educate yourself fully on two things: firstly, on foetal development, which you can freely find on The Endowment for Human Development website[16]. Secondly, inform yourself on what abortion procedures truly look like. Visit the Centre for Bioethical Reform UK website[17] and read up. Look at the images. If you know you absolutely cannot stomach watching a live abortion, then would you, instead, please watch an animated video on YouTube called

[15] Zacharias, R. and Murray, A., 2020. *Seeing Jesus From The East*. Zondervan, p.124.
[16] The Endowment for Human Development - Improving Lifelong Health, One Pregnancy at a Time. *The Endowment for Human Development - Improving Lifelong Health, One Pregnancy at a Time* [online] Available at: https://www.ehd.org/ [Accessed 9 Oct. 2019].
[17] Centre for Bio-Ethical Reform UK. (2019). *Centre for Bio-Ethical Reform UK*. [online] Available at: https://www.cbruk.org/ [Accessed 9 Oct. 2019].

Abortion Procedures: 1st, 2nd and 3rd Trimesters, narrated by former abortionist Dr Anthony Levatino. I won't allow ignorance to be an excuse to anyone reading this book – so that you cannot say you 'didn't know'.

Chapter 3: The suffering question

*"Christianity teaches that, contra fatalism, suffering is overwhelming; contra Buddhism, suffering is real; contra karma, suffering is often unfair; but contra secularism, suffering is meaningful. There is a purpose to it, and if faced rightly, it can drive us like a nail deep into the love of God and into more stability and spiritual power than you can imagine." – **Tim Keller, Walking with God Through Pain and Suffering***

You might have just finished the last chapter, and having duly looked at the grisly truth about abortion, are now feeling any number of emotions – shock, disgust, confusion, ambivalence. You might be feeling a tug of war between what you've seen, and the reality of a world where abortion must surely be a necessary option. Even if abortion is really that difficult to look at; that brutal, that disturbing, surely there are cases where it can be understandable? You think of a woman's suffering, and you think that the world is unjust and unfair enough that abortion must remain a choice, at least in exceptional circumstances.

I've touched on the issue of suffering already in the last chapter, but when it comes to abortion, it deserves to be given a more thorough treatment. Abortion and suffering go hand-in-hand, for suffering is probably the most common and certainly the most powerful argument used for abortion.

It's one of the hardest narratives to disentangle ourselves from as Christ-followers - the idea that abortion is somehow a woman's right or a positive option for even a desperate woman.

But if abortion is as I've laid out in the previous two chapters – the wilful destruction of a human life bearing the image and design of the very Creator of the universe – then this cannot possibly be true.

For even if abortion alleviated women's suffering (and it is highly debatable that it does), how can we justify it when it takes an innocent human life?

Keeping the main thing the main thing

Of course, some of the concerns raised by the pro-choice lobby and well-meaning everyday citizens are valid, especially when they pertain to a woman's suffering. And if you are still on the fence about abortion (or at least about vocally disagreeing with abortion), on the grounds that you wish to spare women from suffering, then I commend your heart. But, and I say this with all gentleness, many Christians have been sadly deceived by abortion proponents' almost sole focus on women, in order to shift away from the humanity of the unborn. We get overly wrapped up in secondary matters, when the primary right to life is the one most urgently at stake. Put as simply as possible, the numerous other concerns raised in defence of abortion just don't matter as much as literal life-or-death.

In 2018, staff apologist for the Life Training Institute Clinton Wilcox reviewed a book called *Trust Women: A Progressive Christian Argument for Reproductive Justice,* by Rebecca Todd Peters. In his review he says: *"Peters' new tactic is to frame the conversation away from what the unborn are and more toward the lives of women. She believes that the complex lives of women are the foundation that we must start from in the conversation on abortion."*[18]

This tactic is common. So it is unsurprising that in my experience writing about or engaging with the abortion issue, by far the most common objection I hear concerns the difficult circumstances a woman may find herself in, where she has 'no other choice' but to opt for abortion.

I have occasionally asked for clarification when such claims are made but do not always get a clear-cut response. When I do, it is usually the rape example. I get that. I don't agree with it, and I'll come to that later, but I understand the heart behind it. And I understand that rape is not the only reason why a woman may feel driven to abortion.

I suspect that it's rather easy as Christians to become sheltered from some of the horrors of life – we can forget that women can be forced into abortions by their families or

---

[18] Wilcox, C. (2018). *Book Review: Trust Women: A Progressive Christian Argument for Reproductive Justice by Rebecca Todd Peters [Clinton Wilcox].* [online] Lti-blog.blogspot.com. Available at: http://lti-blog.blogspot.com/2018/12/book-review-trust-women-progressive.html [Accessed 9 Oct. 2019].

partners, or pressured by medical staff. We can forget that women who are very vulnerable or lacking financial stability may feel that abortion is their only option. We may not have an inkling of the heart-wrenching dilemma parents may face when told their child is likely to have a severe disability. Certainly, when discussing this issue in any context, we must never lose our compassion or our empathy. But so too must we acknowledge abortion cases like this for the tragedies they really are. What kind of society allows a woman to resort to killing her own child because she doesn't know what else to do?

Yet that is exactly the society we have created. Pastor and theologian Dietrich Bonhoeffer said in his unfinished work *Ethics*: *"A great many different motives may lead to [abortion]; indeed in cases where it is an act of despair, performed in circumstances of extreme human or economic destitution and misery, the guilt may often lie rather with the community than with the individual."*[19]

The abortion lobby celebrates 'choice' – much of the debate around abortion, particularly as it pertains to the law, revolves around this word. But what kind of choice is the choice to kill? A woman who chooses abortion due to a real or perceived lack of options is hardly making an empowering choice.

And yet, in 2018, Irish citizens cheered and celebrated as they heard the results of their referendum on abortion. In January 2019, New York State legislated abortion up to birth

---

[19] Bonhoeffer, Dietrich, and Eberhard Bethge. *Ethics - Dietrich Bonhoeffer.* Macmillan, 1965, page number unknown.

if the baby is deemed to die soon after birth, or if the mother's health is deemed to be at risk. The latter is a clever clause totally open to abuse, much in the same way as the 'mental health' clause in the UK is used to justify convenience-based abortion (which counts for around 98% of UK abortions). Third-trimester abortion is not necessary for medical reasons. Yet the legislation was passed amidst cheers and jubilation. Later that day, New York City lit up its landmark buildings in pink as a sign of celebration. They should have been lit up in blood red as a sign of deep mourning.

It may be one thing to gravely accept abortion as a perceived necessity, but how can such evil be applauded?

The answer lies in the fact that society has been collectively deceived. This is unsurprising when we remember that Satan, the Father of lies, hates the human race because it bears the image of God. As I mentioned in the previous chapter, the unborn child has been dehumanised. We've believed the lies and the results have been disastrous.

Months after Ireland voted to repeal the 8th amendment, the nation's citizens were interviewed by pro-life organisation Life Institute about the finer points of the proposed legislation. Many were horrified to find that it would allow abortion up to birth for babies with profound disabilities, that the aborted babies would not be given burial rights, that no pain relief would be given and that babies who survived the abortion would be denied life-saving treatment.

Meanwhile, the Enemy of our souls laughs at our collective folly and our blindness.

There's a particular craftiness about the way we've been deceived about abortion, though. Unlike other injustices where the perpetrator vs. victim is clear-cut, when it comes to abortion, women are sometimes victims too. The suffering that may lead them to have an abortion is real – and this, I believe, is part of the reason why Christians in the UK are characteristically silent on the issue.

Playing moral arbiter

Since rape is the most commonly used example when attempting to justify abortion, I'll address it – firstly by reminding you that abortions because of rape make up a tiny percentage of all abortions. It's easy to get distracted by the rape question when the vast majority of abortions are not performed on these grounds.

Yet I believe it is worth alluding to if only to help you frame a robust and consistent rebuttal to the prevalent narrative. I throw my hands in the air and admit that I have absolutely no idea how devastating it must be to be raped. But I recognise as well as I'm able to that becoming pregnant as a result of being raped must be incredibly hard. I, like every other 'pro-lifer' I've ever met, fully believe that rapists should be duly punished. Celebrated and controversial political and social commentator Ben Shapiro goes so far as to say that rapists should be castrated – it's not a crime to be taken lightly.

I do not believe that abortion is a just answer to pregnancy through rape, nor do I believe that abortion is the answer to a woman's suffering after rape – or any other suffering, in fact. Indeed there is scant evidence that abortion, if defined as the intentional killing of the child, is ever even medically necessary.

I remember an exchange on Facebook after a family friend posted an abortion-related article. One lady suggested in the comment section that women only have late-term abortions in situations where the baby is unlikely to survive outside the womb. Statistics from the Guttmacher Institute[20] (a pro-choice organisation) contradict this statement, so I posted a link to an article[21] where she could read the stats for herself. She responded by arguing that we should do more to tackle the reasons listed, such as poverty, mental health issues and domestic violence. It's difficult to dispute this, of course – no-one would argue that we shouldn't be tackling these things; but there seemed to be this implication that because these women were suffering, we needed to make the alleviation of this suffering our primary objective – rather than the prevention of killing innocent human lives. This kind of detraction from the primary issue at hand seems to be common.

---

[20] Guttmacher Institute. (2013). *Who Seeks Abortions at or After 20 Weeks?*. [online] Available at:
https://www.guttmacher.org/journals/psrh/2013/11/who-seeks-abortions-or-after-20-weeks [Accessed 9 Oct. 2019]
[21] Eunjung Cha, A. (2019). *Tough questions — and answers — on 'late-term' abortions, the law and the women who get them*. [online] The Washington Post. Available at: https://www.washingtonpost.com/us-policy/2019/02/06/tough-questions-answers-late-term-abortions-law-women-who-get-them/ [Accessed 9 Oct. 2019]

Here's the problem: Suffering may lead to wrongdoing, but it does not justify it. The line of argument I see so frequently is that abortion must be an option for women who are suffering. In other words, killing unborn children is seen as the lesser of two evils in certain circumstances.

This is moral relativism and it is dangerous ground to tread. Attempting to justify taking an innocent life is always dangerous, and as Christians, we should know better than to partake in this. No matter how sound our reasoning may appear to our limited human comprehension, it is not our call to decide who lives and who dies.

Clinton Wilcox continues in his review of *Trust Women: A Progressive Christian Argument for Reproductive Justice*: *"By attempting to reframe the discussion of abortion, [Peters] can completely dismiss the question of whether or not the unborn are human beings with a wave of the hand and resort to telling stories about the difficult situations women find themselves in and justifying their decision to abort based on their considerations regarding that difficult decision (of course, she ignores the fact that abortion is only a difficult decision because there is a human child at stake in the decision)."*

He continues: *"One could just as easily support infanticide or toddlercide by arguing that we should reframe the discussion away from one of are infants and toddlers human persons and toward one of the complex lives of parents. However, if the unborn are persons, as pro-life advocates argue, then we can't just take them out of the equation."*

As tragic and as heart-wrenching as human suffering can be, it never grants us the right to inflict death on another as an attempt to escape such suffering. Suffering is part of the human condition – as I mentioned in Chapter 2, Jesus promised us that we would have trouble. It's the inevitable consequence of fallen mankind. But through the cross, Jesus demonstrated that through suffering comes great beauty. We have hope because Jesus Christ took on suffering to give us life. In our suffering-evasive society, it is completely counter-cultural to choose to sacrifice for the sake of another – but it is the way of Christ.

Maybe some of us need to allow God to change our mindset on suffering.

Glory in weakness

There is hope and redemption in a woman's choice to give her child life even when such life was conceived in rape. There is little hope or redemption in adding the injustice of abortion to the injustice of rape.

The same can be said of cases where a child will have a disability or a life-limiting condition. There is hope and redemption in cases like this too. Think of the Australian speaker Nick Vujicic, a man born without arms and legs. God has worked powerfully through Nick, whose life was once dark and full of despair, but is now full of hope and vibrancy. Not only has Nick overcome seemingly impossible odds, but he inspires millions with his message.

Naturally I understand that not every child who is disadvantaged by sickness or disability will grow up to overcome their disadvantages like Nick. They may not boast his many accomplishments; in fact their accomplishments may be very few. They will, like all human beings, experience trials or difficulties. I can't pretend to know what it's like to care for a severely disabled child or relate to the heartbreak of watching your child suffer. But thankfully, God is still God. Life is still life – valuable, worthy of love. The moment we begin to classify which lives matter more or deserve to live more on the basis of ability, we tread far too close to eugenics.

Disturbingly, our very justification for abortion on the grounds of disability is not terribly dissimilar from what the Nazis believed. For the approximate 98% of abortions performed on healthy babies, society claims the choice is beneficial for the woman. But for the 2% of disability-related abortions, society claims benefit to the child; that the child's life is not worth living and so they'd be better off killed before birth.

Adolf Hitler believed in the concept of the 'Lebensunwertes Leben' (life unworthy of life), and used it to justify the mass killing of disabled citizens. In his *Second Book* he praised the Spartans for their practice of selective infanticide, writing: *"The exposure of the sick, weak, deformed children, in short, their destruction, was more decent and in truth a thousand times more humane than the wretched insanity of our day which preserves the most pathological subject, and indeed at any price, and yet takes the life of a hundred thousand healthy children in consequence of birth control or through abortions, in order subsequently to breed a race of degenerates burdened with illnesses."[22]*

Of course, this single quotation alone reveals the true motivation for the Nazis' eugenics programme: it had nothing to do with being 'humane' and everything to do with trying to rid society of what they deemed a burden.

We may not be euthanising disabled adults in the UK right now, but we are seemingly quite comfortable with screening out Down's syndrome, for example. Around 9 in 10 mothers whose unborn children are diagnosed with Down's choose to abort them.[23]

I remember watching a documentary several years ago called *Father of Lights,* where a Christian film-maker follows various ministries across the globe. Though I have reservations about the documentary, one.. particular story deeply moved me: The lives of Mike and Deena Van't Hul. This ordinary American couple felt the call of God on their lives, sold everything and moved to China, where they founded a home for abandoned and unwanted children. Some of those children had severe disabilities; some of them didn't live past infancy. To watch these children simply being held and loved powerfully illustrated the simple and profound value of human life. There was no other justification necessary for the

---

[22] Hitler, Adolf (1961). *Hitler's Secret Book.* New York: Grove Press. pp. 17–18.

[23] The National Down Syndrome Cytogenetic Register for England and Wales:
2009 Annual Report: (2019). [online] Available at:
http://archive.wolfson.qmul.ac.uk/ndscr/reports/NDSCRreport09.pdf
[Accessed 6 Oct. 2019].

worth of those little ones. They were human, and that was enough. As Deena Van't Hul herself stated, *"We believe God is the Giver of Life and that if He chose for a life to be created that there is purpose in the life. And these children have taught us more than probably some of the greatest teachers and preachers of our time about love."*[24]

Merely to witness this couple pour out love on these children is a powerful refutation to the oft-cited excuse for abortion: That if abortion didn't exist, many unwanted children would be born into a world full of suffering. Rephrased: rather than allowing children to grow up sick, poor or unwanted, we should kill them instead. This is so alien to the way of Christ that I am dismayed whenever I see Christians use it as an argument. What if our attitude was, instead, more like that of the Van't Huls?

God is glorified through the lives of the least of these, for God is glorified through our weakness, not through our strength.

---

[24] *Father of Lights*. (2015). [DVD] Directed by D. Wilson. WP Films.

Chapter 4 – A new form of women's oppression

"I understand all the reasons why the movement's prime attention is focused on the unborn. But we can also say that abortion is no bargain for women, either. It's destructive and tragic. We shouldn't listen unthinkingly to the other side of the time-worn script, the one that tells us that women want abortions, that abortion liberates them. Many a post-abortion woman could tell you a different story." – **Frederica Mathewes-Green, 'When Abortion Stopped Making Sense',** *The National Review***, published January 2016.**

There is more to be said on the subject of suffering, and that specifically pertains to the suffering many women experience after abortion. It is highly debatable whether abortion actually alleviates a woman's suffering; instead, evidence would suggest that the contrary is true.

In 2018, nearly 98% of all abortions carried out in England and Wales were listed as ground C – a perceived risk to the woman's mental health.[25] Being poorly defined, this seems to

---

[25] Department of Health and Social Care. *"Abortion Statistics for England and Wales: 2018."* GOV.UK, 1 July 2019,

be used as a clause for abortion on demand, and it's difficult to gauge exactly what negative mental health risks would be posed by continuing with the pregnancy. What is easier to gauge is the negative mental health impact caused by *not* continuing with the pregnancy.

A comprehensive, evidence-based review of the physical and mental effects of abortion on women's health in 2017 concluded: *"While research proving causality is limited, and much research in this field is yet to be conducted, there is already a large body of evidence describing the adverse outcomes. Women are entitled to be made aware of all the associated risks."*[26] The review, conducted by Dr Greg Pike, Founding Director of Adelaide Centre for Bioethics and Culture, Australia, details the range of potential physiological risks from complications during the abortion procedure to an increased risk of preterm birth and postpartum haemorrhage in subsequent pregnancies, following a previous surgical abortion. It also points to studies indicating a higher risk of suicide in post-abortive women in comparison to post-partum women.

Other studies, it notes, demonstrate a link between abortion and adverse effects on women's mental health: *"Numerous studies have identified emotional distress immediately after abortion and in the months following. Women experience a*

---

www.gov.uk/government/statistics/abortion-statistics-for-england-and-wales-2018.

[26] Pike, G. (2017). *ABORTION AND WOMEN'S HEALTH*. [PDF] SPUC. Available at: https://www.spuc.org.uk/publications-library/750-abortion-and-womens-health-april-2017-pdf/file. [Accessed 16 Oct. 2019].

range of emotions after abortion, including sadness, loneliness, shame, guilt, grief, doubt and regret [...] In the longer term, some women exhibited cognitive dissonance, describing their abortions of 10 years or more ago in terms of negative emotions yet believing the correct choice was made. Specific strategies of avoidance were used to cope."[27]

And when it comes to depression and anxiety, the review states: *"Results from a 2006 New Zealand study on mental health and abortion confirm other work showing a link between the two. The New Zealand study revealed that 42% of women who had an abortion experienced major depression in the four years prior to interview. This is nearly twice the rate of those who had never been pregnant and 35% higher than those who had continued their pregnancy. This study also showed that abortion increased the risk of anxiety disorders."*[28]

Though the SPUC review is careful to stress that selection bias and a whole host of other factors make evidence of causality limited, the findings are sobering nonetheless. The review is available to view for free in PDF format on the SPUC website.

In truth, none of these findings should be surprising considering the significance of the act of abortion. The bond between a mother and her child is one of the strongest on earth. To deliberately sever that bond is bound to have repercussions.

---

[27] Ibid, p.21
[28] Ibid, p.22

Neutral NHS?

But the after-effects of abortion do not seem to be common knowledge, and abortion providers certainly do not appear to make full disclosure a priority.

The NHS itself has become increasingly evasive on the subject over time. In 2002, its website stated: *"Physical recovery, especially after an early abortion, is usually quick. You may experience a few hours of period-type pain and a few days of gradually lessening bleeding similar to a period. However, psychological recovery may not be as rapid, as many women suffer from feelings of regret, guilt or depression. How traumatic a woman finds this situation depends on many factors, such as her personal circumstances, the reasons for the termination and how sure she was about the decision to have the procedure done."*[29]

In 2004, it added: *"Many people have very strong views and opinions about abortion (both for and against), often based on deeply held religious, cultural or philosophical beliefs. Whilst all of these views should be respected, the law in the UK makes it legal to have an abortion in the first 24 weeks of pregnancy providing certain criteria are met."*[30]

---

[29]Web.archive.org. (2002). *NHS Direct Online | Encyclopedia | Abortion | Recovery.* [online] Available at:
https://web.archive.org/web/20020820210634/http://www.nhsdirect.nhs.uk:80/nhsdoheso/display.asp?sSection=Recovery&sTopic=Abortion
[30] Web.archive.org. (2004). *Encyclopaedia Topic : Abortion, Section : Introduction.* [online] Available at:
https://web.archive.org/web/20040718080635/http://www.nhsdirect.nhs.uk:80/en.asp?TopicID=1

In 2017 it read: *"Women who have an abortion are no more likely to experience mental health problems than those who continue with their pregnancy."* Not only is this rather a callous dismissal of women who do suffer serious psychological damage after abortion, it also fails to fully brief women on the potential consequences of their actions.

In fact one of the things that sadden me most in this messy and ugly debate is that, many if not most women who walk into abortion clinics are not making a fully informed decision. They are not always made fully aware of their growing baby's development in the womb. They are certainly not given the full breakdown of the process of an abortion.

A quick search on the NHS, Marie Stopes and BPAS websites will confirm this. Surgical abortion is referred to as a 'minor' procedure. Vacuum aspiration abortions are described to 'remove the pregnancy' with 'gentle' suction. In truth, the suction machines used in vacuum aspiration abortions are around 10-20 times more powerful than your household vacuum cleaner. Nothing is said of the dismemberment of the child during these abortions, or of the very deliberate dismemberment that takes place during D&E abortions.

On all of these websites, when discussing abortion the unborn child is referred to merely as 'the pregnancy' or 'pregnancy tissue'. Not even a foetus; just 'pregnancy tissue'. Of course, as mentioned previously, when referring to a wanted child, the language completely changes. A mother going for her 12-week scan is never congratulated on her growing foetus.

The NHS also allows minors to have an abortion without even the knowledge, let alone the consent, of the parents: *"If you're under 16, your parents don't usually need to be told. Information about an abortion doesn't go on your medical record."*[31]

Yet this does not seem to be public knowledge. In January 2019, popular soap *Coronation Street* sparked controversy when it depicted a pregnant 14-year-old being told she could have an abortion without parental consent. Many of the public reacted in surprise and confusion, having assumed that parents must surely be informed about such enormous decisions.

Abortion regret

And what about those women who regret their abortions? Unsurprisingly perhaps, this is also downplayed. After all, once the unborn child has been successfully dehumanised, it's a little inconvenient to offer a platform to those who regret ending the life of their baby. It doesn't really provide a consistent narrative, does it?

In 2017 I read an article on the BBC website which included stories from women who had had an abortion. Many of them described mixed emotions, and strikingly, conflict between

---

[31] nhs.uk. (n.d.). *Abortion*. [online] Available at:
https://www.nhs.uk/conditions/abortion/ [Accessed 16 Oct. 2019].

guilt, and claiming to not regret their decision.[32] Interesting, isn't it, to find such internal conflict and mixed messages. Though society tells women they have nothing to feel guilty about, the guilt or regret remains.

Elaine Storkey comments on the weight of an abortion decision in *Mary's Story, Mary's Song*: "*Pregnancy itself is a symbol of deep hospitality. It is the giving of one's body to the life of another. It is a sharing of all that we have, our cell structure, our blood stream, our food, our oxygen. It is saying welcome with every breath, every heartbeat [....] This is one of the reasons why the decision for an abortion is such a painful and heavy one [...] In spite of all the reasons which directed them to take this step some feel guilty of a deep betrayal of trust. They could not find within themselves the hospitality that was needed to sustain this life.*"[33]

The sad truth is that women are being betrayed by the abortion industry. They too are victims of this injustice. Too many women have been taken in by promises of choice, empowerment and autonomy. Too many women have been shielded from the truth about the life inside them, the way that life is taken, and the fallout of their choice.

This is far from being progressive or forward-thinking. There is nothing civilised about convincing women they should feel no guilt over destroying their own children, and hiding the truth of their choice from them. Women are made in the

---

[32] BBC News. (2017). *From relief to regret: Readers' experiences of abortion*. [online] Available at: https://www.bbc.co.uk/news/magazine-38775641 [Accessed 16 Oct. 2019].

[33] Storkey, E., 1993. *Mary's Story, Mary's Song*. London: Fount, p.34

image of our Creator; it is the most terrible affront to our own nature to destroy the very life we have just created.

If we as believers truly care for the well-being of women (and judging by my conversations with Christians on and off social media about this issue, we certainly claim to), then we have to believe that women deserve better than abortion.

I'm grateful for the airtime given in July 2019 to a young woman named Laura who appeared on the Victoria Derbyshire show amongst a group of panellists to discuss the abortion issue. Laura spoke bravely of her pain and regret – yet also spoke of having since found wholeness and healing. There are so many women like Laura whose voices must be heard, not muffled.

I know that what I've laid out in this chapter is heavy-going. Thank you for sticking with me, especially if you are reading this and you yourself have had an abortion. I can't begin to imagine how tough it must be to work your way through this book, so if that's you, a special thanks for your willingness to engage. It might be a good time to mention that if you have experienced an abortion directly or indirectly, and you want help or support, Post Abortion Support for Everyone[34] (PASE) offers a ministry to facilitate healing and recovery. You can find PASE directly through their website or reach out via their

---

[34] PASE. (n.d.). *Home*. [online] Available at: https://www.postabortsupport.com/ [Accessed 16 Oct. 2019].

Facebook page. The Pregnancy Crisis Helpline[35] will also offer a free, confidential listening ear if you need to talk.

No uterus? No problem

It would be remiss of me to skip onto the heart of this book without first addressing the role of men. Women, although this section is not primarily aimed at you, you may find it helpful nonetheless. And men, please be assured this is not designed to belittle, mock or patronise you, nor is it designed to condemn. I recognise the damage that has been done by radical feminism and its drive to tear down men and lay the blame for every conceivable wrong solely at your feet. I do not aim to add to this destructive finger-pointing.

That doesn't mean you get to be let off the hook when it comes to this topic, though. If we are to see any positive change at all, you need to be included in the discussion.

Please, as you read this, take some time to stop and ask God what He wants to highlight to you about your part in this cultural war.

It must first of all be emphasised, because it is so often overlooked, that abortion can and frequently does cause men deep grief and loss, as it does women. Men, too, suffer as a result of the deceptive rhetoric of 'choice'. Too many fathers have been shouted down when they have tried to

---

[35] Pregnancy Crisis Helpline. (2019). *Pregnancy and Abortion Support - Pregnancy Crisis Helpline*. [online] Available at: https://pregnancycrisishelpline.org.uk [Accessed 16 Oct. 2019].

express the very real bereavement of abortion. 'No uterus, no opinion' is such an empty lie. I remember listening to a radio programme (may have been Radio 4) a couple of years ago, during which several men were interviewed about their experience of an abortion decision. Some of the men said that they had never spoken about it to anybody. I was extremely moved by what I heard. The possibility that this male silence might be commonplace is terribly sad and it highlights the depth of damage abortion causes to all those involved. It also demonstrates the power that pro-abortion rhetoric has had, with men gagged by constantly being told the lie that abortion is a woman's decision concerning her body, and her body alone.

Yet, of course, it would be cruel and deeply wrong to suggest that men should not be held responsible for abortion, when so often, it is man's very lack of responsibility that leads to this tragedy. Think of the women who opt for abortion because their partners leave, or threaten to leave. Think of the men who use women for sex and run before they must face the consequences. In early 2019, the Metro published a feature[36] on six women who shared their abortion experience, and half of them said they'd been coerced into abortion. A selfish, controlling or noncommittal approach to sex and relationships is one of the driving factors behind abortion, and men must acknowledge their part in this. Pro-abortion advocates sometimes raise the issue of men's

---

[36] "Six Women Open up about What It Was like to Have an Abortion." *Metro*, 9 Jan. 2019, metro.co.uk/2019/01/09/six-women-open-up-about-what-it-was-like-to-have-an-abortion-8309559/ [Accessed 16. Oct. 2019]

treatment of women to justify their position, and though there is no justification for abortion, we can appreciate that there is some substance to their point.

A church friend of mine is involved with a charity based in Honduras that helps to build homes and schools, provide livestock and give children a head-start by sponsoring them to attend school. In early 2019 he returned from a trip out there and presented his adventures on a Sunday morning. One thing that struck me was the prevalence of single parenthood there and its correlation to poverty. Sadly, teen pregnancy and single motherhood is commonplace in Honduras because it is so ingrained into the culture. I am not for a moment suggesting that abortion should be introduced as an antidote to this. What I am suggesting is that there is a serious problem in Honduras with regards to how men treat women, and the consequences are on display for all to see.

Single motherhood is prevalent enough in British society as it is. But if we think ourselves more civilised over here because it's less commonplace than it is in countries like Honduras, we should consider that this may be partly because abortion is so often the UK's hidden 'solution' to sexual irresponsibility.

A study by CareNet showed that the father has the greatest influence on a woman who is considering an abortion.[37] We must take the role of men in this debate seriously if we are ever to see a cultural shift.

---

[37] "Abortion and the Church Research." *Abortion and the Church Research*, resources.care-net.org/abortion-and-the-church-research/

Abandoning pregnant women, pressuring them or threatening them into abortion is wrong, that must be clearly understood. But I don't say this to condemn. For the past few years God has placed a burden on my heart for the men of this nation, who so often seem adrift, directionless and devoid of purpose.

John Eldredge writes of the true crisis of masculinity in his New York Times bestseller *Wild At Heart* – and regardless your opinion of his work, I believe he offers some helpful insights into the current climate: *"Society at large can't make up its mind about men. Having spent the last thirty years redefining masculinity into something more safe, manageable, and, well, feminine, it now berates men for not being men."*[38]

But Eldredge doesn't simply point to the influence of radical feminism – the problem is deeper than that, and he goes on to discuss at length the role of the father figure – or lack thereof. Later he reflects on Adam and Eve hiding from God after disobeying Him, commenting: *"We are hiding, every last one of us. Well aware that we, too, are not what we are meant to be, desperately afraid of exposure, terrified of being seen for what we are and are not, we have run into the bushes. We hide in our office, at the gym, behind the newspaper and most importantly behind our personality."*[39]

When it comes to abortion, the concept of hiding is particularly striking. Men may hide behind lust and self-

---

[38] Eldredge, John. *Wild at Heart: Discovering the Secret of a Man's Soul.* Harpercollins Christian Pub, 2011.
[39] Ibid, p.54.

interest rather than have their true nature exposed by the challenge of selfless love, commitment and responsibility. Eldredge posits in his book that *every* man is designed by God to 'come through', yet questions if he 'has what it takes'. A man who is not living in right relationship with God will likely choose to run when things get hard.

Kris Vallotton, one of the senior pastors at Bethel Church in Redding, California, posits that abortion is one of the major side effects of a fatherless culture, in his blog post, '5 Concerning Side Effects of a Fatherless Generation.'[40] I am very cautious of the teachings of Kris Vallotton, but on this issue he does recognise that men have a part to play, and that simply telling women not to have abortions will not adequately fix this cultural problem.

Men who are themselves fatherless in a literal or figurative sense are more likely to shirk the responsibility of fatherhood (while girls without fathers were more likely to become pregnant at a young age). The Centre for Social Justice reported in 2013: *"Young people without fathers are a risk of earlier sexual activity; therefore the children of absent fathers are more likely to become young parents themselves, outside of stable relationships, and repeat the cycle of family breakdown. According to the National Survey of Sexual Attitudes and Lifestyles, children from lone-parent households were more likely to have become sexually active before the age of 16, and girls from lone-parent households*

[40] Vallotton, K. (2019). *5 Concerning Cultural Side Effects of Fatherlessness*. [online] krisvallotton.com. Available at: https://www.krisvallotton.com/5-concerning-cultural-side-effects-of-our-fatherless-generation [Accessed 16 Oct. 2019].

were 1.6 times more likely to become mothers before the age of 18."[41]

So as much as we must show the humanity of the unborn child and reach out to suffering women, so must we address a fatherless culture (a topic that could fill books itself). You may read this as right-wing reactionary rhetoric, but statistics[42] only confirm that God's design for the family was very good and consistently offers human beings the greatest chance of flourishing.

Others have spoken or written at length about addressing both literal and figurative fatherlessness so my comments will be brief.

If you're a man reading this, perhaps you have personal experiences that have been brought to the fore. Maybe you've suffered some loss of your own and maybe you've never spoken of it. If that's you, I'm sorry. I hope and pray that you will find a place to speak of your loss and process it properly – I'll come onto that later.

Or maybe you haven't been involved in an abortion decision but you recognise that you may have behaved in ways that contribute to the culture of abortion in our society. Maybe

---

[41] Fractured Families: Why Stability Matters. (2013). [ebook] London: Centre for Social Justice, p.53. Available at: https://www.centreforsocialjustice.org.uk/core/wpcontent/uploads/2016/08/CSJ_Fractured_Families_Report_WEB_13.06.13.pdf [Accessed 28 Sep. 2019].

[42] "Kids Need a Mom and a Dad – That's What the Research Shows." *Focus on the Family*, 27 Mar. 2018, Available at: www.focusonthefamily.com/socialissues/marriage/marriage/30-years-of-research_[Accessed 10 Sep. 2019]

you've been careless of women's hearts or with their bodies. Do the women in your life trust you to treat them with honour and respect? Do you model responsibility and leadership?

Regardless of whether or not you have children, you can be a spiritual father to the men around you. No matter what your past may have looked like, God can use the contrite and repentant heart. Maybe you have wisdom and experience you can offer to those who are younger or less mature in their faith. Or maybe you recognise that you yourself need fathering. Pray God will reveal Himself to you as Father; the Father to the Fatherless. Pray God would surround you with men who can mentor you and encourage.

Or it may be the case that you're a man reading this and you have persuaded, pressurised or forced a woman into abortion. If that's you, Jesus offers forgiveness freely. He can heal your heart. He can restore all things and He wants nothing more than to bring you to wholeness. It may be that as you take this to God, He prompts you to apologise, if possible, to the woman in question too. Please follow His prompting – it may seem 'too little too late' to you, but you do not know the impact you could have by this simple act.

Chapter 5 - The Church's blind spot

"Where was the Church before Vietnam? Silent. Or there might never have had to be a Vietnam." - **Robert K. Hudnut, A Sensitive Man and the Christ, 1971**

The very heart of this book stems from a deep love of the Church. I was born in the Church and never really left it (to which I can only credit God's grace, the sound teaching of my parents, and the example of some wonderful people). I've been fortunate enough to attend churches of different denominations and a common theme binds them: A desire to preach the gospel and serve their community.

There are so many things the Church gets right and so many ways in which it carries the Lord's heart for justice and restoration. I've seen exciting initiatives to address poverty and homelessness, unemployment, development projects overseas, prison work - even the sex industry and human trafficking. I'm so thankful for and humbled by those who dedicate their time or money to these causes. These people bring Christ to dark places every single day and who make their communities a better place. In many ways they are truly being The Church and fulfilling Christ's mandate to bring justice to the oppressed and set the captives free, as prophesied in Isaiah 61.

But efforts in pro-life ministry have been sadly lacking. Archbishop Justin Welby, to my knowledge, has never spoken publicly to denounce abortion. In July 2019 when the move to impose abortion on Northern Ireland was pushed through the House of Lords[43], not a single Bishop was even present, let alone spoke or voted against the bill.

In my personal experience, abortion has never been preached about from the pulpit. I have heard it mentioned in passing comments, but never in a full sermon, and only once have I heard an encouragement to get involved with or financially support a ministry that sought to protect the unborn and support their mothers. I have almost never heard a call to intercede for the unborn as part of a prayer meeting.

And perhaps saddest of all, I have received little encouragement or support from the wider Church in my own efforts to speak on this issue. In fact, I have faced some rejection for it. I am not saying this to provoke others to pity, but it does no good sugar-coating the truth. From speaking with others who devote their time and energy to defending the unborn, my experience is a common story.

It's common not only anecdotally but statistically. A 2011 survey conducted by the Evangelical Alliance found that there is no clear consensus about abortion amongst

---

[43] Gordon, Gareth. "Peers Back NI Same Sex Marriage and Abortion Reform." *BBC News*, BBC, 17 July 2019, www.bbc.co.uk/news/uk-northern-ireland-49024595?fbclid=IwAR1bg6VP04fCQRfNJqhBfYUWQ_Va6n2xuqd4Wz65K0oN_wGqx3NehTBs6mY [Accessed 16. Oct. 2019]

Evangelical Christians. We do not even hold a consistent pro-life position, let alone act on behalf of the unborn.

The same survey found that abortion ranked 15th on a list of what pastors talk about from the pulpit – on a joint level with climate change and extreme wealth distribution. I have a feeling that by now, that number has dropped lower still. Think about that. To put it bluntly, the mass killing of the unborn is not only not our primary concern – it's considered about as important as reducing carbon emissions. In short, we are ourselves confused about the abortion issue, and our leaders are not doing an awful lot to bring clarity.

A word-search of articles spanning 117 years since the founding of the EA showed a distinct lack in Scriptural and theological engagement with the subject of abortion.[44]

Abortion is undoubtedly our biggest blind spot.

I don't say this to condemn. It is not the first time we have missed something vital.

Both the Protestant and Roman Catholic Church in Germany were virtually silent about the antisemitism and eventual slaughter of the Jews during Hitler's rule. Though there were individuals who were involved in the Nazi Resistance, church leaders as a whole did not speak up about this atrocity. They, too, had been deceived by the promises of Hitler and the scapegoating of the Jews. One of the few notable exceptions

---

[44] Cliff, M. (2020). *"To what extent is there a silence in regards to the issue of abortion within the contemporary evangelical church in the UK?"*. Masters. Middlesex University.

was Dietrich Bonhoeffer, a pastor and theologian, for whom we have to thank for the insightful statement: *"We are not to simply bandage the wounds of victims beneath the wheels of injustice; we are to drive a spoke into the wheel itself."*

At the age of 39, Bonhoeffer was hanged for his bold opposition to the Nazis, only a month before Germany surrendered.

History repeats itself if we let it

Yet Bonhoeffer is not the only one who paid the ultimate price for standing for the oppressed.

Martin Luther King Jr., leader of the Civil Rights Movement which led to the recognition of equal rights for black and white citizens, is considered by most of us to be a hero; a great and courageous leader who also eventually died for his beliefs. He was posthumously awarded the Presidential Medal of Freedom and the Congressional Gold Medal, and some of his speeches are still widely recognised today.

Like Bonhoeffer, Martin Luther King Jr. was a church leader - a Baptist minister as well as an activist. You'd suppose, then, that the Church was on King Jr's side; that the Church fought bravely alongside King to achieve freedom for all.

But the White Church largely ignored King Jr.'s efforts – some even opposed them. In his famous and extraordinarily prescient *Letter from Birmingham Jail*, King writes to church leaders, expressing disappointment over their apathy and urging them to overcome it:

"But despite these notable exceptions, I must honestly reiterate that I have been disappointed with the church. I do not say this as one of those negative critics who can always find something wrong with the church. I say this as a minister of the gospel, who loves the church; who was nurtured in its bosom; who has been sustained by its spiritual blessings and who will remain true to it as long as the cord of life shall lengthen.

When I was suddenly catapulted into the leadership of the bus protest in Montgomery, Alabama, a few years ago, I felt we would be supported by the white church. I felt that the white ministers, priests and rabbis of the South would be among our strongest allies. Instead, some have been outright opponents, refusing to understand the freedom movement and misrepresenting its leaders; all too many others have been more cautious than courageous and have remained silent behind the anesthetizing security of stained glass windows."[45]

Can you imagine being alive at the time of King Jr.? I wish I could say with certainty that I would have been a 'notable exception'; that I would have risked disapproval to stand with King Jr. in his battle against systemic racism. But I cannot. It is more likely that I would have been part of the silent safe; singing hymns to a God that created men equal and free,

---

[45] Africa.upenn.edu. (n.d.). *Letter from a Birmingham Jail [King, Jr.].* [online] Available at:
https://www.africa.upenn.edu/Articles_Gen/Letter_Birmingham.html [Accessed 12 Oct. 2019].

whilst an entire race of people were being oppressed outside the church walls.

The disturbing truth is that in all probability, so would you.

If you don't believe me, consider this: In November 2018, a Christian conference centred on justice issues was held in London. The two-day event included some renowned speakers and covered a range of social issues, including the environment, poverty and ethnicity. The conference website promised to *"wrestle with the burning issues of our time."* Before the conference, my friend Dave Brennan, founder of Brephos, contacted the conference organisers asking whether they would address abortion, or allow space for a stall from a pro-life organisation at the event. After some evasive responses, they finally answered that they would not be addressing abortion because it was too politically sensitive. In 2019, the conference was held for the second time – and for the second time, abortion was not addressed.

Martin Luther King Jr. recognised that neither apathy nor fear was the calling of a disciple. In his letter he speaks of the example of the early Christians:

"But the Christians pressed on, in the conviction that they were 'a colony of heaven,' called to obey God rather than man. Small in number, they were big in commitment. They were too God-intoxicated to be 'astronomically intimidated.' By their effort and example they brought an end to such ancient evils as infanticide and gladiatorial contests. Things are different now. So often the contemporary church is a weak, ineffectual voice with an uncertain sound. So often it is an archdefender of the status quo. Far from being disturbed

by the presence of the church, the power structure of the average community is consoled by the church's silent--and often even vocal--sanction of things as they are."

He could not have known it at the time, but his words turned out to be incredibly prophetic. The words of Dr. King Jr ring as true now as they did then. The only difference is the issue the Church is remaining silent about.

History will repeat itself unless we learn from it.

Outcomes are up to God

Hindsight shows us that the Church's silence on the issues of antisemitism and of racism was wrong, and equated to complicity. Whether or not the ending of these injustices would have been hastened by the Church's intervention is actually beside the point.

The Church must speak primarily because it is wrong to see evil and not oppose it. Philosopher Edmund Burke famously said that the *"only thing necessary for evil to triumph is for good men to do nothing"*. The outcome, though hopeful in light of the history of social reform, is not in our hands – remember Esther's words as she decided to confront the King about the plot to exterminate the Jews: *"If I perish, I perish"*. (Esther 4:16).

This is why I do not accept that fighting to end abortion should be left solely to politicians or to the tiny number of pro-life activists.

Seeking justice, my friend Dave Brennan says, is a command of God, not an optional extra. The Bible commands us to love our neighbour (Matthew 22:39); to *"speak out for those who cannot speak for themselves"* (Proverbs 31:8); to *"Learn to do right; seek justice. Defend the oppressed. Take up the cause of the fatherless; plead the case of the widow."* (Isaiah 1:17).

Of course, our primary mandate is to preach the gospel, but this does not excuse washing our hands of the injustices we see around us.

If we apply these verses to some social issues but not others, we are not being fully obedient. I'm not suggesting we should stop confronting other issues, such as poverty, or drug dependency, or trafficking. But if we do all of this and think that excuses us from addressing abortion, we're mistaken.

Of course, it's unrealistic to suggest that every church must achieve an equal focus on every issue – that would be pretty much impossible. I do believe that God calls different churches to make specific issues their priority, due to their demographic, the area in which they operate, or a whole host of other reasons.

But abortion is simply too great an injustice to ignore on the basis that it doesn't 'fit the programme'. If we tackle everything but abortion, at best, we are inconsistent, and inconsistency is not a good witness to those in the Church and to those without. At worst, we are hypocrites, claiming a passion for justice and the things of God, but cherry-picking only what suits us. I would go as far as to say that silence on abortion renders our other efforts a little hollow. You see, what we say about the unborn underpins our value of all human life. The theologian Francis Schaeffer said: *"Of all the subjects relating to the erosion of the sanctity of life, abortion is the keystone. It is the first and crucial issue that has been overwhelming in changing attitudes towards the value of life in general."*[46]

It starts in the womb; it starts with the most vulnerable. If we demonstrate no value for the unborn, do our efforts towards vulnerable adults ring true? Can we truly speak on the behalf of the poor, the marginalised, the disabled and the oppressed if we will not speak for the most vulnerable of all?

More disconcertingly still, some of the other injustices that the Church has been vocal about are actually helped or spurred on by abortion. For example, sex traffickers rely on easy access to abortion to ensure that their girls keep working if they fall pregnant. These girls therefore have no way out of their lifestyle and the 'evidence' of the traffickers' crimes can be easily disposed of. Moreover, abortion clinics themselves may be complicit in these crimes. In January 2017, it came to light that Planned Parenthood had failed to report several instances of underage sex trafficking. Who knows how many more cases like this have gone undetected and whether similar instances are occurring in the UK?

In 2020 the cry for racial justice was again echoed across much of the Western world following the murder of George Floyd by a white police officer. Many churches spoke out against Floyd's death and engaged in many conversations about racism more generally. Indeed the topic of racism has

---

[46] Koop, C. Everett., and Francis A. Schaeffer. *Whatever Happened to the Human Race?* Crossway Books, 1984.

filled numerous books and no doubt will fill many more. But are we aware of the racist roots of the USA's Planned Parenthood? Do we know that Margaret Sanger, one of PP's founders, was a eugenicist who wanted to decrease the African American population? Consider these lines in a letter she wrote in 1939 to Clarence Gamble: *"The most successful educational approach to the Negro is through a religious appeal. We don't want the word to get out that we want to exterminate the Negro population, and the minister is the man who can straighten out that idea if it ever occurs to any of their more rebellious members."*[47] Such attitudes ought to wake us up to the depth of depravity that lies behind the introduction of legal abortion.

Do we know that in the Unites States, the abortion rate is still disproportionately high amongst the African American community? That in New York City, more black babies are aborted than born?[48] Would our discussion and tackling of racial injustice be as effective as it could be if we did not acknowledge the significant blow to the African American community caused by abortion?

Simply put, the effects of abortion are wide-reaching and intersect other serious justice issues. Trying to address them

---

[47] Nyu.edu. 2001. *MSPP / Newsletter / Newsletter #28 (Fall 2001)*. [online] Available at:
<https://www.nyu.edu/projects/sanger/articles/bc_or_race_control.php> [Accessed 15 June 2020].
[48] Riley, J., 2018. *Let's Talk About The Black Abortion Rate*. [online] WSJ. Available at: <https://www.wsj.com/articles/lets-talk-about-the-black-abortion-rate-1531263697> [Accessed 15 June 2020].

without addressing abortion seems akin to trying to put out a forest fire with a garden hose.

If your church is one that has been largely silent on this abortion, now is the time to take action. What can we learn from the words of Dr. King Jr.? It is not too late to change the course of history. It is not too late to repent.

Chapter 6 – 'Life and death are in the power of the tongue'

"Not to speak is to speak. Not to act is to act. To do nothing when a house is burning is to do something. It is to let the house burn." - **Robert K. Hudnut, *A Sensitive Man and the Christ*, 1971**

Our own obedience is and must remain the primary matter, but we also know and serve a God who wants to use us to bring change to a world starving for truth and crying out for justice.

We should never underestimate the spiritual significance of speaking truth.

Almighty God created the Universe through the power of His Word. He spoke, and it was. We are created in His image, so although our words do not hold creative power in the sense that we can 'call things into existence', I believe they are still significant. "Life and death are in the power of the tongue", Proverbs 18:21 tells us, so we have a responsibility to use our words wisely. For example, when we worship God with our mouths, we are not just singing words, we are declaring the truth of who Jesus is. When we affirm the value of all human life as sacred, we do not speak in vain. Rather, we counter lies with truth, rehumanising the dehumanised.'

Some reading this may consider the above to be a bit airy-fairy, but the idea of words having a performative function is not new. In his book *How to Do Things with Words,* language philosopher J L Austin described the concept of 'speech acts', which both *say* and *do* something – such as a minister marrying a couple. The speech both communicates and performs.

The Church is a prophetic voice to the culture. Roy McCloughry writes in his book *Living in the Presence of the Future: "[Christians] are a voice of prophecy to the world. We are to be uncompromising to all that is contrary to God's purposes, whether poverty, debt slavery, moral evil or social decadence. Christians are therefore called to be a voice of prophecy, of resistance in an unjust society, and this may sometimes mean declaring that God is judge of the world."*[49] To speak truth to power is our calling the outcome is up to God.

The Church speaks light into the dark places. The Church intercedes for our communities, our nation and our world. Yet the Church has largely failed to fulfil its role as a prophetic voice when it comes to abortion. Is it any wonder, then, that Francis Schaeffer once remarked that every abortion clinic should *"have a sign in front of it saying 'open by permission of the Church'"*? Is it any wonder that abortion is so common; so accepted today?

---

[49] McCloughry, R., 2001. *Living In The Presence Of The Future*. Leicester: Inter-Varsity, p.18.

Silence creates a vacuum. In the absence of a counter-voice, evil ideologies can easily take hold.

It's time to break the pattern of silence in the Church. I am convinced that if we want to see an end to the injustice of abortion, the Church *must* find her voice again, and speak with the authority of Christ both to the congregation, and to the culture.

Facilitating healing

There are many reasons why ending this long silence is vitally important, and one of them is the health and well-being of your own congregation.

I fully recognise that speaking out after 50 years of relative silence is no easy feat. As somebody remarked to me in early 2019, many don't want to *"stick their heads above the parapet."* Abortion is sensitive. It's not as easy to address as it is to address poverty, for example. Poverty is universally acknowledged as wrong. Talking about poverty is not likely to cost you popularity.

In contrast, abortion is not universally acknowledged as wrong, and to speak against abortion is considered by many in the UK to be a disgusting and heinous crime. Not only is opposition to abortion contrary to the status quo, it's also a bit close to home. Abortion directly or indirectly affects members of your congregation. If 1 in 3 women in the UK will have an abortion during their lifetime, it follows that some women in your congregation will have had an abortion.

My highlighting this is in no way meant to condemn those women; quite the opposite, in fact. As I laid out in the previous chapter, abortion is not justifiable but it is understandable – especially when we consider the complex factors that lead a woman to such a choice.

But I once heard it summed up with great clarity. *"Silence from the Church on the abortion issue communicates one of two messages: That abortion is permissible, or that it is unforgiveable."*

Women who have had an abortion – for whatever reason - need you, the Church. They need to know that what they did was a sin – but that they can be forgiven. As I also touched on in the previous chapter, so do the men and any other involved parties.

These women need healing. Remember that many women who have had abortions are plagued with guilt over what they have done and may even suffer a range of mental health disorders including anxiety, depression and even suicidal thoughts.

A 2015 study from U.S. organisation CareNet sheds some sobering light on the effect of the Church's silence on American women, and it can be reasonably assumed that some of this will apply to the UK as well.

Some of the findings are as follows:

Amongst American women who have had abortions, only 4 in 10 believed that the church was a safe place to talk about pregnancy options. Three quarters of women surveyed indicated their local church had no influence on their decision. Half of women believed that a pastor's teaching on forgiveness did not apply to abortion. Half believed that churches do not have a ministry in place to help women with unplanned pregnancies.[50]

Unfortunately, to my knowledge, there has been no UK study of this kind. But making the assumption that the situation in the UK somewhat parallels that of the U.S, there's no doubt that there is room for improvement.

Only God can heal the human heart, it's true. But what are churches if not facilitators for such healing to take place? A woman who has had an abortion needs people surrounding her, walking her through a process of restoration. So does a man who has been involved in an abortion decision – particularly if he has been told repeatedly that his voice does not matter; that his own grief is invalid.

We offer ministry to all kinds of people in all kinds of distress. We must be willing to help post-abortive women and hurting men in our congregations, too.

Silence is not neutral

But there are other reasons why church leaders must speak about abortion.

---

[50] Resources.care-net.org. (2019). *Abortion and the Church Research*. [online] Available at: https://resources.care-net.org/abortion-and-the-church-research/ [Accessed 12 Oct. 2019].

In 2011 The Evangelical Alliance conducted a survey to find out what evangelical church-goers believe about the abortion issue. In answer to the question, 'abortion can never be justified', respondents answered as follows: 20% said they agree a lot, 17% agreed a little, 18% were unsure, 28% disagreed a little, and 17% disagreed a lot.[51]

Evidence shows that church-goers themselves are unclear on the abortion issue. Simply put, we are not united. We cannot even congratulate ourselves for holding a consistent pro-life position. Far from being a clear voice to the culture on what God thinks about abortion, we don't even have consensus among ourselves.

Silence dampens, smothers, muffles and confuses. Silence sends an unclear message not only to the wider world but to your own congregation – is abortion OK? Is it sometimes OK and sometimes not? Or is it too evil to even speak of?

Leaving something in the dark does not make it disappear. The darkness feeds it; the darkness is where it grows. In the absence of clear biblical teaching from the Church, members – particularly young or new Christians – will simply adopt the secular worldview on abortion. The objections I have heard from Christians to the pro-life stance have sounded pretty much identical to the arguments used by non-Christians. And this is almost inescapable – I can recall several separate instances of 'choice' rhetoric spouted by guests on BBC news

---

[51] 21st Century Evangelicals. (2011). 1st ed. [PDF] London: Evangelical Alliance. Available at:
https://www.eauk.org/church/resources/snapshot/upload/21st-Century-Evangelicals.pdf [Accessed 28 Sep. 2019].

– even shoehorned into seemingly irrelevant conversations, such as discussions around Brexit. Like it or not, there is no neutral ground in the ideological sphere. Even to sit on the fence on abortion is to encourage its existence, because only clarity, conviction and action can ever hope to end it.

Church leaders, by speaking to your congregation about abortion, you will equip and empower a generation that will rise to end this injustice. Speaking about abortion will also mobilise your church community to be moved to act on behalf of unborn children and vulnerable women.

Something I hear often is that not enough support is given to women in crisis, either emotionally or practically. This is a vital opportunity for the Church to fill a gap and be the hands and feet of Jesus to pregnant women who require help.

Blessing from obedience

But there is a still more significant reason to break the silence on abortion and it has to do with the collective blessing that comes with collective obedience.

We'd all love to see revival in this nation. We'd love to see our churches full of people hungry for God. We want to see Jesus transform our communities, our cities. Many of us pray for such an outpouring.

If we are being disobedient to God by remaining silent on abortion, will God pour out the full measure of His blessing? Could it be that our silence has been a hindrance to revival – and will continue to be so until we repent? Let us go back to the way God responded to the Israelites tolerating child sacrifice to Molech: He promised to turn His face away from them (Leviticus 20). In Ezekiel 20:31 the Lord says: *"When you offer your gifts--the sacrifice of your children in the fire-- you continue to defile yourselves with all your idols to this day. Am I to let you inquire of me, you Israelites? As surely as I live, declares the Sovereign LORD, I will not let you inquire of me."*

We serve a God who does not change and I truly believe that God will hold to us account for our silence. But I believe with equal conviction that God is ready and willing to wipe our collective sin from His memory the moment we acknowledge it before Him.

We are all familiar with 2 Chronicles 7:14 where the Lord says to Israel: *"If my people, which are called by my name, shall humble themselves, and pray, and seek my face, and turn from their wicked ways; then will I hear from heaven, and will forgive their sin, and will heal their land."* Whatever our beliefs about whether we can apply this passage to our own nation, I do believe there is a case for mass repentance for our ongoing sin of silence, apathy and complicity.

In whatever state we find ourselves - from the pastor who has faithfully spoken out against abortion for decades, to the church member who has never even thought at length about the issue - let us join in collective repentance for the silence of the last 50 years.

If you're a leader or a member of a church that does speak on abortion or are involved in some way in pro-life work, I'm so grateful to you. I pray God will bless you for your obedience. If that's you, please pray for those who have not yet spoken up. Maybe you know someone you could pass this book along to. Maybe you can ignite passion in others to join you in engaging with this issue.

Chapter 7: What happens if we don't speak?

*"Fools said I, you do not know! Silence like a cancer grows." – **The Sound of Silence,** Simon and Garfunkel*

If the last chapter offered a picture of hope for the Church and society if we end our silence on abortion, this chapter will inevitably provide a sobering picture of the alternative. I do not write this to monger fear or to prophesy doom and gloom. Jesus has already won; one way or another, all evil will one day end as He returns in glory.

However, God desires to use us to bring change. The current trajectory can be altered if we partner with Him in what He wants to, through obedience to His Word.

But what if we don't? What if we, as the body of Christ, continue to sit back and watch as the enemy wreaks havoc upon this nation?

The truth is that none of us know. Just as other social injustices have been ended with frankly little co-operation from the Church, it may be that abortion is eventually exposed for the evil it is and outlawed. But it may not be. King Jr. said in his *Letter from Birmingham Jail* that *"time itself is neutral; it can be used either destructively or constructively. More and more I feel that the people of ill will have used time much more effectively than have the people of good will."[52]*

Let us not forget that the very concept of human rights is founded in Judeo-Christian principles. Think of the Declaration of Independence: *"We hold these truths to be self-evident, that all men are created equal, that they are endowed by their Creator with certain unalienable Rights that among these are Life, Liberty and the pursuit of Happiness."* Britain's Magna Carta, which was established in 1215, assumed that the nation's law must be subject to God's law. Or to go further back still, fourth-century Church Father Gregory of Nyssa described slavery as an institution that violated humanity's creation in the image of God – one of the first to criticise the practice of owing slaves. History demonstrates that in the Western world, we have developed our understanding of human rights from the values taught in the Word of God.

It's easy to make some educated guesses as to where we may be headed if we continue as a nation to drift from that foundation.

We can almost guarantee that abortions will continue all over the country at a similar rate to the stats of recent years; indeed, if abortion is introduced in Northern Ireland, this

---

[52] Africa.upenn.edu. (n.d.). *Letter from a Birmingham Jail [King, Jr.]*. [online] Available at:
https://www.africa.upenn.edu/Articles_Gen/Letter_Birmingham.html
[Accessed 12 Oct. 2019].

number will be higher still. That means over 200,000 more unborn children will continue to be killed every year; 200,000 more precious lives known and loved by their Heavenly Father. That means more women and men will be seriously affected by abortion, wounded and scarred by the act of extinguishing life; men and women who spend the rest of their lives carrying this pain.

But there are reasons to believe that the situation could get even worse. In the UK, radical proponents of abortion are pushing to allow women to have abortions on demand – up to birth, for any reason. New York State recently passed legislation to allow this, and The British Pregnancy Advisory Service, the UK's leading abortion provider, is spearheading the 'We Trust Women' campaign which has the same end goal. BPAS CEO Ann Furedi admitted in February 2019 that the New York bill is *"what many of us have been campaigning for in the UK"*.[53]

We were asleep when abortion was snuck into Northern Ireland in 2019. If we continue sleepwalking we will end up with exactly the kind of 'free-for-all' scenario BPAS is pushing for.

Let's not forget that abortion is already permissible up to birth in the case of disability. And statistics show that the

---

[53] NRL News Today. (2019). *British abortion boss: Extreme New York bill "is what many of us have been campaigning for in the UK" - NRL News Today.* [online] Available at:
https://www.nationalrighttolifenews.org/2019/02/british-abortion-boss-extreme-new-york-bill-is-what-many-of-us-have-been-campaigning-for-in-the-uk/ [Accessed 12 Oct. 2019].

number of late-term abortions in the UK is on the rise. In early 2019, Sir John Hayes asked the Secretary of State for Health and Social Care how many abortions had taken place after 20 weeks each year for the previous five years. The answer showed that the number rose from 2,753 in 2013 to 3,564 in 2017 - an increase of 30%. The total of abortions at this late stage in the last five years was 14,996.

There are already places where abortion on demand is legal, such as in Canada, and in Queensland, Australia. Can we imagine living in a nation that tolerates this? Do we want to allow ourselves to join them in this darkness?

Not slopes, avalanches

What's troubling is that those who push such extreme laws seem to be unaware of how close their position is to infanticide – or if they're aware of it, they simply do not care. And why *should* they note a distinction? After all, deep down they know that the child does not suddenly obtain human rights once it passes through, as I've amusingly heard it termed, the 'magical birth canal'.

Of course, there are some ethicists who are least intellectually honest and logically consistent enough to recognise that there really is no moral difference between abortion and infanticide, most notably Peter Singer, who in 1975 argued that parents should be able to euthanize disabled infants.

If, like Singer, the population adopts the secular, Darwinist view of life (and without the Church, it will), then infanticide may slowly become socially acceptable – at least, to begin with, for the sick or disabled.

And what then? If killing newborns becomes permissible, what about the elderly or the sick? In the Netherlands, assisted suicide and euthanasia account for around 4.5% of deaths. Once considered a compassionate solution to terminal illness for the elderly, now people in the Netherlands are being euthanized for dementia and mental health conditions. In Belgium, children with terminal illnesses are being euthanized. Pro-euthanasia campaigners mocked the 'slippery slope' argument yet it is exactly what transpired; in fact, it was more like an avalanche than a slope.

In 2020 a disturbing story surfaced in which the court ruled that a 34-year-old man's life support should be removed – despite giving informed consent to a surgery that would have been life-saving. The man had earlier indicated he did not want to live with a stoma bag but later changed his mind – yet his life support was turned off anyway.[54]

The more permissive our abortion law becomes, the more likely it is that we will begin to treat the elderly, sick or otherwise vulnerable in a similar manner.

---

[54] Hussain, D., 2020. *Patient, 34, Dies After Judge Ruled He Had Right To Refuse Stoma Bag*. [online] Mail Online. Available at: <https://www.dailymail.co.uk/news/article-8405789/Patient-34-dies-judge-ruled-right-refuse-permanent-stoma-bag.html> [Accessed 15 June 2020].

Let's go back for a moment to the plight of the disabled. How will we begin to treat them if our culture further devalues life? Although we currently live in a society that seems to value the less able-bodied among us, we also live in a nation where 9 in 10 babies who are diagnosed with Down's syndrome are aborted. 15 unborn children were killed last year simply because they suffered from a cleft palate – a condition easily corrected by surgery. If abortion is seen as totally morally acceptable, at any stage and for any reason, why shouldn't aborting the disabled be considered a convenient escape from the burden of caring for them? Why shouldn't eugenics be viewed as a gift to society? Why not create 'designer babies'?

Our laws will become increasingly inhumane – just consider the Irish bill that withheld pain relief to the unborn and ruled that victims of failed abortions would be left to die. Similar laws are in place in some U.S. states.

In June 2019 came the chilling ruling that a woman with learning difficulties would be forced to abort her 22-week-old baby.[55] The ruling was made despite protests from the woman's mother, a former midwife, who promised to take care of the child, and indications from the woman herself that she appeared to want the child, although she reportedly did not have the mental capacity to make her own decision. The judge claimed she was acting in the best interests of the woman.

---

[55] Sky News. (2019). *Woman with mental age of child to have abortion, court rules*. [online] Available at: https://news.sky.com/story/woman-with-mental-age-of-child-to-have-abortion-court-rules-11746576 [Accessed 12 Oct. 2019].

Thankfully, after a mass outcry against this decision, it was revoked. Yet if we have so successfully dehumanised the unborn that such a suggestion was made in the first place, this may well be the kind of callous state intervention we might expect in the future. Indeed in October 2019, a similar ruling was made after another woman with learning difficulties was found to be pregnant. The circumstances differed slightly in that it was suspected that the woman may have been raped and reportedly has not expressed any reaction to the pregnancy. But for such a ruling to be made – the second in the matter of months - is concerning. As Christian charity CARE pointed out[56], it demonstrates the state of society that we consider abortion a just solution with no regard for the life of the unborn, for the potential long-term consequences for the women or even for her bodily autonomy.

If we do not consistently speak of the intrinsic worth of every human being created in the very image of God, why shouldn't the culture adopt a pragmatic, utilitarian or aesthetics-based approach to value? Remember, there is no neutral ground when it comes to ideology. There is truth or there are lies.

The availability and frequency of abortion also creates a vicious cycle. Often caused by casual sex and uncommitted relationships, it also fosters it, perpetuating its own culture.

---

[56] CARE. (2019). *Forced abortion returns: Judge orders abortion on woman with learning disability*. [online] Available at:
https://care.org.uk/news/latest-news/forced-abortion-returns-judge-orders-abortion-woman-learning-disability [Accessed 16 Oct. 2019].

As long as abortion is considered an acceptable option (and some women do consider abortion as just another form of birth control), men and women will continue to seek pleasure without purpose, and avoid pursuing the permanent, exclusive and life-giving covenant of marriage. I am not saying that the end of abortion will itself end this crisis of dysfunction, but the continuation of abortion will surely exacerbate it.

Time and time again we as the Church have recognised that the family is the foundation of society, and the cost of family breakdown is huge. Continuing to fracture the family unit will increase brokenness and devastation across our country, and future generations will suffer the consequences.

Chapter 8: Law matters

"The fundamental basis of this nation's laws was given to Moses on the Mount...If we don't have a proper fundamental moral background, we will finally end up with a totalitarian government which does not believe in rights for anybody except the State." — **Harry S. Truman**

You may be wondering where the law fits into all of this. After all, morality may be one thing, but the law has the final say. Amongst Christians there seems to be a diversity of opinion on whether we should be focusing our efforts on outlawing abortion - with some believing this is absolutely imperative, and others believing we have no place trying to influence public policy in a secular society.

My personal conviction is that laws both reflect and influence the social climate. On this particular subject, I believe in focusing on changing both the culture and the law, as the law should be a natural progression of a shifted collective mindset. I also believe there is a case for arguing that the law influences culture in turn.

Laws matter and I do not think attempting to influence the law is itself wrong. Laws set a precedent and a clear boundary as to what a nation will and will not tolerate.

Morality is not neutral, and so laws communicate a nation's embrace of moral good or moral evil. On such an enormous topic as abortion, then, it's crazy to think that Christians should just stay out of all matters legal and let the secularists dictate.

I think of the way Argentina responded when a bill seeking to legalise abortion was defeated in 2018. The joyful celebration from the crowds thronging the streets was absolutely beautiful to witness even through my little iPhone screen. Not only did it stand in stark contrast to the way the Irish cheered upon the repeal of the 8th amendment, but it reminded me that our law in the UK is extremely liberal in comparison to other nations.

There may be those who believe abortion is wrong, but would not want the law to prevent others from making that decision. But in what other circumstance would we be against legislating morality? Rape, theft, assault and homicide still occur despite being very much illegal. Common sense and a concern for the protection of society prevent us from ever being tempted to legalise such crimes.

So whilst reiterating that I am more interested in seeing a total culture shift than merely making abortion illegal, I do think the legal debate forces us to confront the issue.

Safe, legal and rare?

In 2019, the USA saw a spate of pro-life bills signed into law, protecting life from its earliest stages. This caused an enormous backlash with all kinds of ridiculous claims about men trying to legislate against women's bodies (even though the governor of Alabama is, in fact, a woman), and how making abortion illegal will only drive it underground.

Do you remember when Hillary Clinton said in the 1990s that she wanted abortion to be *"safe, legal and rare"?* Of course, 'safe abortion' is an oxymoron – abortion is never safe for the unborn child, nor is it risk-free for the mother. But more pointedly, such a statement sounds completely alien now. Since abortion was made legal in the United States in 1973, abortion rates have skyrocketed. Similarly, in the UK, there were around 28,000 abortions in 1967, compared to 200,000 in 2018[57]. Legalising abortion increases rather than reduces its occurrence.

Of course, to an extent, some women will choose illegal abortion. But there are many examples of countries where abortion rates are low because it is still illegal. Northern Ireland is a good example: Around 100,000 people are alive today because the nation staved off abortion for the last 50 years.[58]

Additionally, also contrary to popular belief, making abortion illegal does not always increase maternal mortality. After abortion was criminalised in the 1990s, maternal mortality rates dropped in Chile, Poland and Nicaragua. Even in El

---

[57] Johnstonsarchive.net. (n.d.). *Historical abortion statistics, United Kingdom*. [online] Available at:
http://www.johnstonsarchive.net/policy/abortion/ab-unitedkingdom.html
[Accessed 12 Oct. 2019].
[58] Both Lives Matter. (n.d.). *Both Lives Matter*. [online] Available at:
https://bothlivesmatter.org/statistics [Accessed 12 Oct. 2019].

Salvador which has a high number of illegal abortions, fewer pregnant women died following the criminalisation of abortion in 1998. Meanwhile in South Africa, maternal mortality rates actually rose after abortion was legalised in 1997.[59]

Others claim that pro-lifers only care about children before they're born, and that if abortion were made illegal, more children would grow up in poverty or other types of suffering such as the care system. Instead, some argue, Christians should concentrate efforts into alleviating poverty. In other words, unless Christians singlehandedly end all the factors that drive women to abortion, we are not worthy of the label 'pro-life'. Of course, such reasoning is flawed. Not only are many Christians involved in supporting crisis pregnancy centres and new mothers, but many Christians already work hard to help alleviate poverty and suffering. Yet abortion still exists. Why? Simple: because it's still an option. Making abortion illegal would eliminate or at least severely restrict the option, forcing society *as a whole* to work harder to resolve the underlying issues. In a wealthy, developed nation like the United States, there is no reason why this shouldn't be a tangible goal to work towards. In fact, by keeping abortion legal, we are allowing it to act as a sort of unseen 'pressure-valve' for all manners of other serious social issues. As I touched on in Chapter 5, problems such as teenage sex,

---

[59] Hogan, M., Foreman, K., Nagavi, M., et al. (2010). *Maternal mortality for 181 countries, 1980–2008: a systematic analysis of progress towards Millennium Development Goal 5*. [PDF] Lancet. Available at: https://www.thelancet.com/action/showPdf?pii=S0140-6736%2810%2960518-1 [Accessed 16 Oct. 2019].

fatherlessness, rape, prostitution and sex trafficking are all propped up by abortion: it provides a means for these acts to continue and in some cases even helps to prevent their detection.

Alabama and Georgia, as well as the extreme pro-abortion bill in New York, pushed the topic into the public space once again in 2019. Law and culture necessarily go hand in hand, and I believe that what is decided in the United States will eventually trickle down to other Western nations, including the United Kingdom. It may not appear that way as I write this in July 2019. As mentioned in passing a few times throughout this book, the pro-abortion lobby successfully tacked an amendment onto a Northern Ireland bill that instructs the Government to provide for a repeal of sections 58 and 59 of the Offences against the Persons Act. In simple terms, this would effectively legalise abortion in Northern Ireland. Not only is this undemocratic and an abuse of power, as abortion is a devolved issue in Northern Ireland, but it's unwanted. A 2018 ComRes poll showed that two thirds of women in Northern Ireland did not want abortion to be imposed upon them[60]. And this says nothing of the devastating contrast to the way Northern Ireland has protected the unborn up until now.

These may seem like dark days and it may be difficult to envision a shift. Yet this is exactly why we must act. I truly believe that it has never been so vital for the Church to speak

---

[60] Comresglobal.com. (n.d.). [online] Available at:
https://www.comresglobal.com/wp-content/uploads/2018/10/2018-Both-Lives-Matter.pdf [Accessed 12 Oct. 2019].

on this issue as it is now. Like Esther, we are here for 'such a time as this'.

It may be difficult to imagine Parliament outlawing abortion the way Alabama and Georgia have in 2019, but let's be thankful for the shift in the United States and pray it continues, that it might force us as a nation to confront the morality of this issue head on.

If we are serious about provoking discussion about abortion as a cultural problem, in time I believe we will see the law shift too.

Chapter 9: The Strategy of Heaven

"When God has something very great to accomplish for His church, it is His will that there should precede it the extraordinary prayers of His people." – **Jonathan Edwards**

The previous chapters have been heavy and doubtless hard to digest. If for any reason you have gotten to this chapter and your spirit is heavy, downcast and full of doubt, please know this is not the heart of God. The magnitude of this problem may seem intimidating but fear is not of the Lord.

Don't be disheartened - God is greater. We can see an end to abortion and I believe that we will; for some of you younger readers, maybe even in this lifetime. You are alive for such a time as this. So if you are feeling that heaviness, shake it off. There's work to do and God wants you on your feet.

I hope to share some practical suggestions as well as some things I believe the Lord has shown me over the course of the past year or two.

Pray and fast

The first point is something everyone can do. It costs you nothing but your time and maybe any remaining apathy;

Prayer, Fasting, Intercession. Things change when God's people pray.

A lady at my parents' church likes to use the example of George Mueller, who established an orphanage in Bristol in the 1800s. Throughout his lifetime, Mueller cared for over 10,000 orphans and opened 117 schools. Mueller never asked for financial support, instead relying completely on God to provide. The rent was always paid; the children never went hungry. I am always awed by hearing of Mueller's life. Imagine having this kind of faith. Imagine if we prayed with this kind of dependence and expectation.

I believe there has been a marked lack of serious corporate prayer and intercession over the issue of abortion in our nation, and though I believe the body of Christ is starting to wake up, there are many of us who are still sleeping. A couple of years back I caught a repeat of a 2017 conference in Florida. Lou Engle, a Charismatic church leader, was speaking. Lou Engle founded the large prayer and fasting movement The Call, Whilst I disagree with Lou Engle on some theological points, I was amazed at his extraordinary passion and conviction over abortion, the likes of which I have not seen here in the UK. We cannot afford to be lax about this; to be apathetic, passive or flippant. If this is the most pressing human rights issue of our time (and I would argue that it is), then we should be devoting a lot more time to address it in our church meetings, marking out time to cry out on the behalf of those who can't. It's simply too important to sweep under the rug because some church members may find it uncomfortable. Human lives are being destroyed. Are hurt feelings really of greater concern? When you stand before

God one day, do you think He will ask you what you did to protect the feelings of your flock or your fellow church members? Or will He ask you what you did for the least of these?

Individual prayer is also vital in this – God certainly hears the cries of His intercessors and Heaven is moved to act on behalf of our petition. If we are serious about ending abortion, prayer is our go-to; our first and last step and every step in between. I say this as much to myself as to you.

How do we do this? Where do we even begin?

Firstly, reminding ourselves that this is a spiritual battle is paramount. It's no good framing abortion as just another moral issue. It is, frankly, demonic at its core, in the same way that child sacrifice to Molech was thousands of years ago. Please understand the distinction I am making here between human beings who, one way or another, find themselves making the decision to have an abortion, and the actual evil behind abortion itself. As I have stated in the first chapters of this book, we have been deceived by the Enemy of our souls. We must pray accordingly. *"For our struggle is not against flesh and blood, but against the rulers, against the authorities, against the powers of this dark world and against the spiritual forces of evil in the heavenly realms."* (Ephesians 6:12)

I say this only to help us remember to maintain perspective – that we would trust always in God's sovereignty, and that in our righteous anger we would have compassion on those perpetrating the evil of abortion, knowing that only God can bring them out of darkness. Keeping these things in mind, these are some specific points you can pray into.

Pray for the protection of the unborn; that their destinies would not be thwarted; that they would live to glorify God. Pray for women in crisis pregnancy situations, that their hearts would be turned towards their child and that they would be connected with the right support. Pray that they would be informed of the reality of the choice they are considering. Pray for fathers to rise up with courage to protect their partner and their child, and to choose responsibility for their actions.

Pray for those who work in abortion clinics, that God would soften their hearts and draw them to Himself. Pray for influential leaders in the abortion industry such as BPAS CEO Ann Furedi, and MPs like Stella Creasy and Diana Johnson. Pray that, leaders like Furedi may have a radical change of heart like that of former Planned Parenthood worker Abby Johnson, whose experience has inspired the hit 2019 U.S. movie *Unplanned*.

Pray for those who work or volunteer for pro-life organisations and for those who stand in public spaces/outside abortion clinics to pray or minister – for strength, protection, wisdom and strategy. Pray that as a collective Church body, we would repent of the part we have played in allowing this to continue for so long. Pray for your own church leaders, that they may have the grace to tackle this issue with boldness and with sensitivity. Pray for the emergence of more voices like Esther to intercede on behalf of the unborn – particularly those of women, including women who themselves have experienced the trauma of abortion. Pray for MPs who are pro-life, that they would have opportunities to advocate for mothers and children alike, with unwavering conviction.

Pray for a collective awakening to the reality of an abortion and for a mass turning of hearts. Pray for a great exposure of the abortion industry for what it is. Pray that our society, which has lost its belief in the intrinsic value of humanity, would begin to promote a culture of life. Pray for a wave of adoption and fostering to be one of the radical, practical moves of God's people to counter this crisis.

Pray for an end to abortion in this nation. Pray that the scales would fall from the eyes of each man, woman and child in this nation and that they would see abortion with a clarity that sees through the lies of 'choice' and 'healthcare'. Pray that one day the citizens of this nation would look back on abortion in the same way that we look back now on the horrors of Transatlantic slavery and the Holocaust – unthinkable, never to be repeated. Pray that the justice of the Lord would come and that it would come swiftly.

Pray that we will see a shift in our broken, fatherless culture; that that we might see the Lord, as in Malachi 4:5, restore the hearts of the fathers to their children and the hearts of the children to their fathers"

Give

This one is as practical as they come and hardly needs to be prayed or chewed over at length. Give your money and/or your time. The pro-life movement is small. It needs resources if it is to have a greater impact. What do you have to offer that could help spur this movement forward? Skills which you can volunteer? Do you have counselling skills you could offer to a crisis pregnancy centre? Are you an excellent organiser or administrator? Do you have finances that can go towards a pro-life charity of your choice? Or perhaps instead, you could contribute to a grassroots effort in your own church community to provide expectant mothers with practical support? I've seen initiatives to donate practical items to the homeless: Could you also start up similar banks for expecting or new mothers? Could you donate baby clothes, nappies, toys?

Equip

It may be that you are fully convicted that silence is no longer an option, but, layman or church leader, you have no idea where to even begin. The good news is, there are resources out there. To book a talk in your own church, reach out to Dave Brennan of Brephos, a ministry that was created for this exact purpose. Visit brephos.org for more information or for previous talks you can use as resources to equip yourself. The Gospel Coalition website offers various sound articles on the subject and there are several good books to help you fully grasp the pro-life position and argue for it solidly. *The Case for Life* by Scott Klusendorf or *Why Pro—Life?* By Randy Alcorn are both good and accessible options. Check out Vaughan Roberts' new book *Talking Points: Abortion.*

Although US-based, Live Action is a great organisation to follow online for a larger awareness of the abortion industry and strategies to defend life. The Life Training Institute and the Equal Rights Institute are both excellent resources for pro-life apologetics. Follow CBR UK on social media and check out some of the training material offered. And for an intensive apologetics crash-course, sign up for CBR UK's next *Clarkson Academy*.

Share

One of the simplest things you can do is raise awareness. Start with your own friends and family. I've had such brilliant conversations with friends that have stemmed from my pro-life beliefs – some of whom have then considered the abortion issue for the first time.

Write to your MP and ask them where they stand on the issue. When abortion related bills are presented in Parliament, ask them how they are intending to vote. Urge them to defend life.

If you use it, take advantage of social media. I know: 'like, comment, share and subscribe' are four words most of us are probably sick of hearing; yet in this bottomless pit of information we call the internet, certain topics and figures do rise to prominence through the phenomenon of exponential growth (aka, 'going viral').
Anyone remember 'KONY 2012'? I was university when this video campaign came out and spread like wildfire amongst the Facebook feeds of my peers. Since the whole thing was

pretty roundly debunked it's become a distant memory (and if you're not of the millennial generation, you probably won't remember it at all, since the PEW research centre reported that *"younger adults were also more than twice as likely as older adults to have watched the video itself on YouTube or Vimeo"*[61]).

A more recent example would be the rise to fame of 16-year-old climate change activist Greta Thunberg, who appeared before the UN in September 2019 to berate them for what she believed to be a failure to act to protect the planet. The availability of social media meant that it was pretty much impossible to avoid Greta and her message (regardless of what you or I thought of it). Naturally, sharing and commentary of the clip by people on both sides of the debate followed shortly afterwards. Being confronted with the issue forced people to think about it, even if merely on a surface-level, knee-jerk reaction kind of way.

Why does this matter? Well, examples like this support a trend that's been demonstrated over and over again: That young people learn, share and are strongly influenced by social media. Like many, I have a love/hate relationship with social media: there are times I wish I could delete Facebook forever, but I recognise its advantages when it comes to the spread of ideas. The very act of making a 'taboo' subject open to discussion creates scope for minds to be challenged and changed, and when it comes to abortion it is vital that

---

[61] Pew Research Center: Internet, Science & Tech. (2012). *The Viral Kony 2012 Video*. [online] Available at:
https://www.pewinternet.org/2012/03/15/the-viral-kony-2012-video/
[Accessed 12 Oct. 2019].

we confront our culture with the issue. If there were greater numbers of people – particularly of the younger generation – beginning to speak out and question the accepted narrative, we would almost certainly see a shift in public opinion. A recent video from CBR UK which showed the reactions of members of the UK public, after being shown a video of an abortion, reached over 1.2 million people on Facebook and has been watched over half a million times.[62] Virtue-signalling is off-putting and it's not enough to merely 'like and share' – but it's a start.

Adopt

Some of us may feel led to larger commitments in our stance for life, including the call of God to take the radical step of fostering or adoption. I do feel the need to stress here that adoption will not solve the abortion problem on its own, nor that we are only pro-life in word and deed if we take on this enormous responsibility.

But there is something about adoption that speaks particularly of the mercy and kindness of God: *"He defends the cause of the fatherless and the widow, and loves the foreigner residing among you, giving them food and clothing."* (Deuteronomy 10:18); *"A father to the fatherless, a defender of widows, is God in his holy dwelling. God sets the lonely in families…"* (Psalms 68:5-6).

And so the apostle James urges us to do likewise: *"Religion that God our Father accepts as pure and faultless is this: to*

---

[62] https://www.facebook.com/163177836133/videos/550909428976249/ get ref

look after orphans and widows in their distress..." (James 1:27)

But there is yet greater theological significance in adoption, for in choosing, claiming and loving those children who have been labelled unwanted, a burden and without belonging, we are demonstrating the very gospel. We are echoing the heart of our own Heavenly Father, who *"predestined us to be adopted as his sons through Jesus Christ, in accordance with his pleasure and will . . . "* (Ephesians 1:5).

We too, alienated and fatherless, were chosen and made sons and daughters instead of orphans. In the act of adoption we demonstrate to the world the meaning of being called, chosen and loved. To a desperate nation, showing the Father's love in such a self-sacrificial way would certainly be an extraordinary witness.

Work

Lastly, it may be that some of you reading this believe that God is calling you to go further still and go into pro-life work full time. There may be some sacrifice in that, it's true. It may mean a pay cut; a loss of social status and reputation. But if the call is from God, you can be sure the joy will outweigh the cost by far.

One phrase in particular, from Gregg Cunningham of CBR in the U.S, really stuck in my mind: *"There are more people working full time to kill babies than there are to save them."*

What would it look like if more Christians prioritised this issue when it came to their career choices?

A culture of life

I've tried to cover a lot of ground in this book and no doubt I have done it imperfectly. My hope and prayer is that something will have resonated with you; that there will be at least one step of action that you, personally, can take.

If you are a church leader I especially pray that you will act upon what you have read. Don't hesitate to reach out to brephos.org if you want to further explore bringing this topic to your congregation. If you are not a church leader, there are still so many ways in which you can join this movement to bring the injustice of abortion to an end.

Change is possible with a persistent voice that will not go away. History shows us that if enough advocates speak out for the voiceless, for long enough, their humanity will again be recognised. And we do not speak feebly or ineffectually. We have help. The same Holy Spirit that raised Jesus from the dead is alive in us. We have creative solutions to the broken mess we are surrounded with. We are to bring light into dark places; we are to speak life over a culture of death. We are to *"expose the deeds of darkness"* (Ephesians 5:11).

As the body of Christ we are the counter-culture. *"The creation waits in eager expectation for the sons of God to be revealed"*, Paul writes in Romans 8:19. Across denominations, across political persuasions and cultural backgrounds, let us be united on this front.

There has never been a more crucial time than now to collectively find our voice and engage our hands and feet. May Almighty God train our hands for war and our fingers for battle (Psalm 144:1). May He teach us to speak with grace, seasoned with salt (Colossians 4:6).

May the Lion of Judah roar over His Church and wake her up, so that in time, we will see abortion become unthinkable.

Lightning Source UK Ltd.
Milton Keynes UK
UKHW031411180322
400276UK00008B/1780